DESEGREGATION, THE EXTINCTION OF "BLACK PEOPLE," AND THE BIRTH OF THE "NORTH AMERICAN"

Published by Spines
ISBN: 979-8-89569-783-2

DESEGREGATION, THE EXTINCTION OF "BLACK PEOPLE," AND THE BIRTH OF THE "NORTH AMERICAN"

A MEMOIR OF LARRY FERGUSON

CONTENTS

Dedicated to Pops looking like a "North American" James Bond

INTRODUCTION

The desire to maintain a status quo uses the oppression of a human as a primary tool. This oppression it's like an absurdist play that's been running far too long, and I'm one of its bewildered actors. Picture this: I'm caught in a fog of sleep, panic rising, convinced I'm late for some vague job I can't even remember. I blurt out, "Hey Google, stop the alarm!"—only to wake up to the harsh, unrelenting reality that I'm just idling at a stoplight. Time stretches and distorts; minutes feel like days, melting into a haphazard existential crisis. I realize at this moment, this strange epiphany, that I'm in the midst of some cosmic metamorphosis, a chaotic creature forged from the mixed-up mishmash of humanity we call North America. Emerging from this metaphorical cocoon? It's an unavoidable truth. Yet there are forces out there, shadowy figures, who want me, and those like me, to remain caterpillars—easy to squash, kept small and silent, stripped of our essential humanity. They've been enforcing this oppressive script for their own gain since the inception of this land. And if we rewind the clock to 1965, the very year I stumbled into existence, we see the critical turning point of their cruel narrative. Life is both a tragedy and a comedy and in this plot twist, I refuse to play the victim any longer.

This is the author's true story of how the final stage of court-ordered integration of North Americans (aka blacks) and Americans (aka whites) in the late '70s thru '80s shaped the values, strengths and ideas as education was no longer preserving the status quo and became the catalyst for change. The effects continue to move through us all as the most volatile virus that is killing off the discrimination and inequalities born from the needs of Americans to oppress the North Americans for the purpose of ensuring their survival and denial of ownership of this land by the oppressed... The results culminate into the place we call The United States of America.

The critical issue at hand is not merely the fear that the illiterate and morally bankrupt among us might seize too much power; rise to prove they are neither illiterate nor degenerate, fully equipped to challenge the system. Like every war, there are factions; each side employs its strategies. Those standing against civil rights will be referred to as "The D.E.A.D"—an acronym for their Devoted Efforts Against Desegregation. This narrative chronicles the maneuvers of both sides, laying bare the number one weapon in the arsenal of the civil rights movement. This weapon is akin to an atomic bomb in its potential for transformation; it is called "Desegregation."

Just like the Iceberg that sank the "Titanic," the virus created by desegregation is killing off the things called hatred, entitlement, oppression and racial inequality, unlike anything we have ever witnessed since the days of Christ. The results are a new body of a man and woman release to the world from this North American cocoon.

Please immerse yourself in personal accounts in this story and draw parallels between what I've experienced and what you've faced in your own life. The diverse rhetoric chronicles my life. Now, here's the crux: the rollout of this integration didn't just ruffle a few feathers—it ignited a tempest of violence and hostility from every conceivable angle. The spark for what I term "The D.E.A.D" came not from a single threat but from a three-pronged attack orchestrated with a disturbing synchronicity—far removed from the monolithic narrative often associated with the civil rights movement championed by Dr. Martin Luther King Jr. As you go through my experience, consider this your forewarning: it's not an addendum to King's legacy but the by-product of North America herself

The integration of blacks and whites was clearly on the horizon. The DNA of the stolen people of Western Africa brought to America is tolerated and not celebrated due to fear. After 600-plus years of evolving, the results of this frustration in the demand for freedom were many, including suicides, the birth of gangs, court-ordered desegregation even a new form of communicating one's feelings through poetry called rap. Some areas of the country implemented desegregation better than others and Cleveland, Ohio was one. The results had a profound effect that resonates throughout the entire world today. These successes formed a virus and for the virus, failure was not an option. Thus, the end of the desegregation experiment was brought about swiftly, by any means necessary and by a variety of groups including the same courts which enacted them. The age-old long tactics of division for the purpose of conquering was the core weapon of "The D.E.A.D." But it has proven to be no match for the virus. But not without millions of casualties.

The Presidency of Barack Obama owes a debt of gratitude to this experiment, for without its trickle-down effect, he would not have won. The fallout still lingers today as many seek to turn back the hands of time to maintain a status quo, and as such, this spearheaded one of the most divisive presidential campaigns in the nation's history with the "Let's Make America Great Again" rhetoric. This story comes from a man who was blessed to endure this time period in what he now knows was beyond the experiences of most and unifies the experiences of many for a time period that a vast majority does not want to recognize existed. In the eyes of the majority, we were simply interlopers, and the aim was to create a world where our existence, both here and abroad, felt like a borrowed illusion, resulting in a populace adrift.

The equality that we give to all mankind is identifying them based on the land mass from which they are made. Understanding the factual importance of the creation of males and females since the first Africans arrived in America in 180 years before Columbus even made his voyage is vital. The DNA of the children of the oppressed is that of a wide variety of human mixtures that span over a 600-year period. The North American cocoon has developed a uniqueness with its blending DNA so that it has its own physical, mental and emotional beings, created only in this its motherland, thus granting its children title by nature. No more the tagging of that of pets, but a respectful title like those given to all the other human beings on earth cocoon from their land would be acceptable as a for of equality. So forgoing the title of "North

American" will be used in this story in lieu of the digration of being called merely a Crayola title or spanish term negro/negra (phonemes substitution NIGGER) for black, meaning black, dark, raven and gloomy. To the degree that it is understood that the calling of a Native American "Red" of "Redskin" is degrading, it should be understood that calling me "Black" or "Nigger" is also degrading. I am a "NORTH AMERICAN".

SIX-FIVE SIXTY-FIVE BORN WITHOUT A HOME

BLOODY SUNDAY

Bloody Sunday took place on March 7th, 1965 in Selma, Alabama. Around 600 people were attempting to cross the Edmund Pettus Bridge to begin the march to Montgomery. Protesters were violently attacked by state troopers.

Alabama state troopers swing nightsticks to break up a civil rights voting march in Selma, Alabama, on March 7, 1965. John Lewis, front right, of the Student Non-violent Coordinating Committee, is put on the ground by a trooper.

om and Pops are watching the news while Pops massages her belly with the top dawg me inside. The stress of the times was crazy during the year I was cooking in the oven. On the 7th of March 1965, known in the history books as "Bloody Sunday," some 600 people began a 54-mile march from Selma, Alabama, to the state Capitol in Montgomery. The nerve of them goddamn niggers, who do they think they fucking with? They think they got protection, yawl get on the phone and tell everyone to meet me at nine you know where.

The black folks were commemorating the death of Jimmie Lee Jackson, who had been shot on Feb. 18 by a state trooper while trying to protect his mother. Here them mother fuckers come, I don't care all of them are coon monkey bastards, got no home and want to fuck up ours. Who got the dogs? Ok. Then, unlike anything you could have thought of, the massacre began. This is Alabama mother fucker, The pictures speak for themselves. "Shit, some are getting away shooting the coons let the dogs out."

That was the catalyst that President Johnson would need to get the "nigger bill" passed. That was his personal name for what we now call the Voting Rights Act of 1965. With the 1964 Civil Rights Act and the 1965 Voting Rights Act, the segregationists would go to their graves knowing the cause they'd given their lives to had been betrayed.

Nonetheless, those who opposed the civil rights movement vowed to overcome this betrayal, and the war for their self-preservation began with a take-no-prisoner mentality. All of this rhetoric was simple: past slavery was not the issue. Plain and simple, they pushed the agenda that these people are creatures and less than human, totally unequaled, and less intelligent than dogs. My dad was to believe, as he was holding me, that I was equal or less than a dog. When I say sit, sit.

It was believed that "North Americans" would be so happy with the things that appeared to be going their way. That many would just roll with that flow. Well, that's exactly what went into play. The flow created a false sense of security. The flow that gave value to fake material goods. The flow created fake senses of belonging to create a deadly feeling of entitlement. There will be no real role models for the new game, so niggers will just follow the fads and have no family.

This was the world my parents thought about right before having to introduce me to the world. It becomes clear why so many succumbed to vices and why men flitted from one woman to another, lost in a dizzying dance of fleeting pleasures. It was a fervent bloom of ego, where self-absorption blinded them to the greater tapestry of life, obscured by towering trees labeled money, sex, and drugs.

Many sought the approval of others, sacrificing their own self-worth in the process. Each decade unfolded like a chapter in our narrative, reflecting the evolving spirit of our journey in tandem with shifting artistic genres. The integrity of our message carried through the arts of the 60s and 70s, became a runaway locomotive, responding to the clamor of the selfish. Their ultimate aim was to persist in tolerating us, viewing "North Americans" not as equals but rather as mere resources vital to their endeavors

My father, a soul touched by this very struggle, often spoke of a man named Winston Willis. A pool hustler hailing from Alabama, he was a man who refused to bow to anyone's will. The path to prosperity was clear for those who were willing to see, and Willie possessed a profound understanding of it, utilizing his knowledge with unmatched skill. He became the archetype for countless "North American" (black) men navigating the streets of Cleveland during the transformative era of the late 1960s and 70s. Ruthless yet resolute, he stood tall against the oppressive forces of police, judges, banks, and, yes, even the very fabric of systemic racism. His accolades were many, bearing titles such as "The Black Howard Hughes," "Cleveland's Porno King," "The Pied Piper of Euclid Avenue," and "105th and Euclid's Slick Young Landlord." Thus, it was at this stage that the men who would profoundly influence my formative years were inextricably linked to the legacy of Cleveland's own Willie—known affectionately as W.E.W. Let us not forget the power of example in our pursuit of justice and equality.

GHOST AND POPS

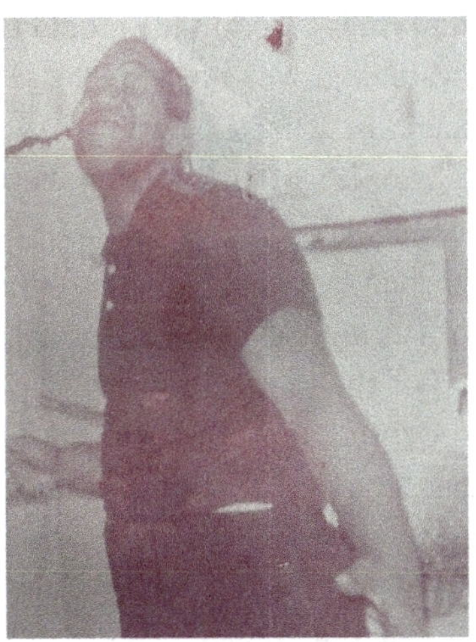

Hey, baby, I'm home. Oh, oh, here come Pops being corny again. He would always tell my mom, "I got the chocolates, so bring that cream so we can make a sundae." I am 50 now and finally get it. Hey, Pops, those corny lines do work. Taking after you, I got four kids now. Anyway, my parents were like most parents of the 60s and liked to get it in.

By now, there were three of us: me, my older sister Bonita and my younger brother Tony.

For some reason, I was just a tad different. Pops said it was because I was two people born a year before the devil, which made me a saint. I said he had some corny saying. But I always tried to find some understanding behind them. For this one, all I could come up with was being born on two numbers, 6-5-65 and during Gemini month. Maybe if he had waited a year later, it would have been 666. What I do know is Pops was really connected to the ideals of freedom, as passed on to him by his father, who was a native of the Bahamas.

The ideal of not being able to be free in every endeavor of life was not an option, and he, along with my uncles, made sure we knew that. He would tell me the spirits of shark food, known as slaves and their blood that watered the palm trees of the Island were watching over me at night. They were under the bed and in the closet, don't be afraid. As much as he was trying to ease my fear, it was just over my head, and I still lay scared at night.

Us kids knew when it was time to go to bed. I would look at Bonita, she looks at me, I'd look at Tony and all I can hear is the opening music of the television show The FBI. Man, they start moving to the room. It's a bedroom we all share together, just a bunk bed, the dark hardwood floor and the closet with crystal eye door knob. Dude, not me. I'm going to watch the FBI; the lights on the TV are safer than that old, dark, haunted room. I know the boogie man in the closet. That's on them.

They were kind of behind and did not get the idea that when Pops was talking about chocolate and cream, we had the TV and refrigerator to ourselves. So peace, I'm staying. Next thing I hear is the playing of the national anthem; shit, it's going to make that sound; I quickly move towards the TV, too late. It was like that long 'BEEEEP' after the national anthem, which was an alarm clock for my mamma to come to check on her babies. Even chocolate and cream had to take a second seat to that. "Didn't I tell yawl ass to go to bed" Woo, mamma knew how to swing that belt?

So now I'm in this room with the boogie man in the closet and the wolfman under the bed, and I'm just awake watching their shadows watching me, just waiting for me to move. It ain't gonna happen. I'm gonna just lay here like a log. Tick, Tock, Tick, Tock time is just wasting away, and then it happens. "Ahhhh, mamma, damn, how did they get into my dreams? Why do they keep at me? Where do they want me to go?" I am just four years old, and I am just as still as a rock, just waiting for those African spirits to come chase the monsters away.

A year later, It's time to go to bed. I am a bit older now. Pops is still talking about making a sundae with chocolate and cream, and my brothers and sis keep saying they want a bowl, too. Anyhow, here comes the music. I look at Bonita, she looks at me, I look at Tony and all I can hear is the opening music of the FBI. The next thing I hear is the national anthem being played. 'BEEEEP.' "Didn't I tell yawl ass to go to bed?"

Now, I have graduated from the belt to the extension cord. Dam, it hurt, but this was when my Ghost showed up. I wanted so badly to scream out I hate you. I had heard that a lot on TV when someone did not like what another person was doing to them. I don't know how this happened, but as I was lying there still as a log, hiding from the shadows of the boogie man and the wolf. It was like I was in two places at the same time. I don't know how, but I was in my mom's room. There she was, half crying. There was no one else there but her. I could see the radio on the floor that used to have an extension cord connected to it. No pops, though. Then the Ghost looked at me. Its face was half body, half something else somewhat mystic. Shit, maybe Pops was right about those

African Spirits. Somehow, I was the third party in the room, and I could see both me and the Ghost. Then I heard a sound say, "See."

I was the first up the next morning and was sitting at the table eating my Cheerios and sugar water when Pops came in. This was a first, but hey, what do I know? He did not see me at first. I watched him come in with his police uniform, which I now know was a security guard uniform with a big badge, and then I saw the strangest thing that did not make sense to me till years later. Instead of taking off his big belt, he put it on. Now, initially, I just had an ah-ha moment of oops, I am sorry, mamma, because I thought she hit me with the extension cord because she wanted to hurt me more, but I see it was because she just did not have the belt. Then it got even stranger; he made sure everything on him was neat, and then he went in the room with my momma and just flat-out forgot. I couldn't believe he had forgotten about sundaes, no chocolate and cream. Alright, Ghost, I trust, and I will always protect my mamma, and as I looked at all the whelps on my legs from the extension cord, all I could think about was my mamma better be ok, don't make me Jimmie Lee Jackson.

ADDITIONS AND SUBTRACTION

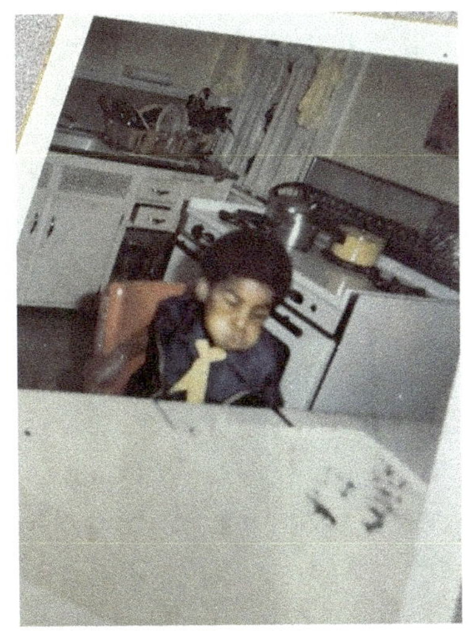

Pops and us all chillin' at the gas station. Man, he had the greatest job in the world. I got to eat all the peanuts and jelly beans I wanted. His gas station was right in the middle of East Cleveland. I thought he owned it but later found out he just managed it and was proud to be one of the first "North American" gas station managers around so he said he owned it.

I'm gonna be better than Willis. Pops would say. He was working two jobs and was never home. He looked out for us, though; even got us a babysitter named Pauline. She was really nice and would also take Pops to work and pick him up after watching us. For some reason, I had not seen much of my mom since my birthday party, but hanging out with pops was cool, except it was just me.

Now, I know I am just four, but leaving me at this gas station, just me and a worker all the time, just wasn't cool. Then, one day, here comes Pops rolling up with a pink blanket in hand, momma in the car. Funny though, she didn't get out of the car, but he brings this shriveled up red looking thing over to me. "Junie," that's what they had begun to call me, "this is Tabitha." I quickly said, "That ain't Tabitha, she white," thinking of the baby on the television show "Bewitched". He said, "Boy, no, your little sister." I paused, thought about it, then looked a little closer. Man, if this wasn't the prettiest thing I had ever seen. Jet black head full of hair with cheeks just like mine. Yep, she's mine, I can tell. Those are my cheeks. I'm gonna let nothing happen to her promise. I remember saying. Then we went home.

Pops began to work more, trying to be better than Willis. I still didn't get it, though. Pops was the man to me. Shit, my uncles are better than Willis. I really thought my Uncle Buddy was the man. That's my momma's brother. He was the owner of Dexter's Barber Shop in East Cleveland just down the block from the Winton Willis row of businesses, and my uncle Bobby was rich, he had a house with a pond that had fish, and he had a pool table too. But I'm stuck in this gas station because of Willie. Summer vacations were supposed to be fun and I was stuck at the gas station.

Well, summertime is gone. Now, it's 1972, and I started school at Mayfair Elementary. I was already more mature for my age and was always listening to grown folks' conversations.

I often heard folks say that Willis was a jive pimp. So I questioned why my pops wanna be a pimp. I learned that language from the television shows "The FBI " and "Flip Wilson Show " and the kids in school that's how they talked. I thought it was jacked up, but it seemed like all they were doing was being mean to each other, talking bout each other's momma and playing like they might beat you up.

It was crazy how in those days, first graders could walk the neighborhood by themselves. One day I was crossing the field behind the school and stumbled across a pocket knife. Now, the only time I have seen one was on the FBI. Man, I ran home with it, and then it started to talk to me. No, for real, it talked to me. It was like "You know I will protect you," and "You know what they made me for" "If somebody hurt you, let me help you." I am not joking; this thing was talking to me, so I had to check myself. Ok, I look around and no one is in the room. My mouth is not moving, so I am not making a sound. Where are these words coming from? Ooh, it's the "The D.E.A.D"s. trying to get me. Ok, I am going to just chill.

I woke up the next morning, feeling the weight of the day ahead like a fresh page waiting to be filled. As I stepped outside, the air felt electric, calling to me, whispering, "Hey, you can't just leave me behind." I dashed back into the house, slipped it into my pocket—an unspoken bond between us— and hurried to school. We understood each other, always ready with words, no misunderstandings, no conflict. But on the way, a few guys fell in step beside me, their laughter echoing with the confidence of youth. They started with that game of the dozens, a pastime I never quite grasped. Maybe it was my sense of honesty, but I believed words had power. When someone speaks, they reveal their truth—or they lie.

Then one of them aimed his barbs at me. "Yo momma so black her butt look like two tires!" The laughter surged around us. "Yo momma so fat and black she looks like a burnt marshmallow!" Their rhythm was relentless, striking like the flames of the arena. "Yo momma so black, when she talks, shit comes right out her mouth!" And it went on. "Yo momma so black she's the reason we're scared of the dark." Each line felt like a dart, but I stood resolute. "Yo momma so black," another chimed in, "when God made her, he said, 'Damn, I burnt one!'" My patience began to wane, but I didn't know them, their lives, their stories, their mothers. I was trapped in this elaborate game, so I finally yelled, "Shut the hell up." They halted, a wall of challenge blocking my path. "Why, what you gonna do?" one taunted. I could feel the anger rising, threatening to spill over. "Don't let another word slip out," I warned. But then it came, the last blow, "Yo momma so black she don't know who her daddy is, and neither do you!" And just like that, they sprinted off to school, leaving me to ponder the weight of their words and whether I would ever find the courage to stand up against the hunger for belonging.

All day I was like, "Shut up," "No," 'I ain't' "Shut up," "Nope," to my new friend, then I started to cry. I was so mad or hurt I began to listen to my new friend. He had a plan, and that put a smile on my face. See, I didn't like this feeling, and if I didn't want to feel this way again, well, you know. School is over, and I am full of anxiety even have a smile on my face. I ran the first block of the way home, knowing this would put me ahead of the crew. Just like clockwork, when they saw me ahead of them, they ran to catch me. I could hear them coming, as they could never do anything without laughing. By the time they caught up to me, I could hear they were out of breath.

Then one opened his mouth, still tired from running, "Yo Yo ma". Before he could get another syllable out of his mouth, my new friend said, "Now." I whipped that pocket knife out so quickly and with just one swoop of my arm at his chest. I missed my best friend missed. It was a miracle, and they all took off running home to their dark-ass mommas. Now, if I am writing this story, then you know the next day I lived, but ooooh, did she kick my ass. How could someone whoop you so long crying the whole time? She cried more than me. I even heard her crying the next morning. I try to remember the rest of my time in the 1st grade, and all I can come up with is a blur; I realize she beat me so bad I lost nine months of my life. She was a victim, too. The "The D.E.A.D" 's plan to divide the family was done exactly for this reason. I was shot. I tried to kill someone. But I survived as the dudes were still alive, and momma didn't catch a case for beating my ass. I know she did it for me, and today, I still love her for it. We win, they lose.

Pops, on the other hand, didn't lay a hand on me. He said it was his fault, "I fucked up, and now they winning", referring to "The D.E.A.Ds. I was like ok, he ain't beat me cool, so I said, "I'm sorry, Pops." Then he got mad and taught me something that I carry on today. He asked me, "What are you sorry for?" I told him, "because I did something wrong." He then said, "Boy, never say you sorry for doing something wrong, did you get the feeling you want to get from it?" Now, I was thinking to myself, what was he talking about? He then yelled, "Get that funny look off your face. Did you feel good when the boys ran?" I said, "Yes." "Then you are not sorry for it. Was it wrong?" I said, "Yeah". He then went on to explain that I need to apologize for my actions, not get into my feelings, and learn how to play chess, not checkers.

You are a colored kid and will be a colored man, and sometimes we have to do things and it might not make people feel good. What you should use when you have done something wrong is "Apologies" instead of "Sorry". I got confused again, but this time, he just touched my chin and explained. "Play chess, not checkers. Always control your feelings before you speak because you can never take away words that come from your mouth. The ears that receive those words will take what you say as the truth. So, son, are you sorry?"

I quickly answer not. He then told me, "Your ears heard something different and believed the person that said it. So, who said you were sorry?" I answered I did. He then asked me, "which one is the truth, or are you lying to yourself?" I said, "Oh, I get it. It's for when you have not done something well." He then nodded. Oh, I did well with what I wanted to do and ran and now they will leave me alone. But I hurt people in the process, so I must apologize. Yes, son, he said always try not to be self-destructive. There are too many other things out there trying to tear you down, so please don't do it to yourself, no matter how small. Those boys let a small thing like comedy almost ruin a lot of lives. Your freedom is a vote for your people; that's what people before you died for. So, if you guys don't commit suicide, you can win and live better than us. You guys got to be more serious and clown less, you haven't been through enough to need the medicine of comedy. That went way over my head. It took almost 20 years before I understood it, but I never forgot it. So, till today, I don't say I'm sorry. But I will apologize. This goes over most people's heads. That was the last one-on-one conversation I had with my pops for 12 years. The bullet of temptations the D.E.A.D. fired hit my pops. Pauline was more than a babysitter; she was his woman, and Mom was not having that, so they split up.

WOMEN ARE STRONG TOO, UMM

While I was going through these growing pains the adults of my day were getting caught up in the perks of that thing called freedom the " DEAD" folks were teaching them. It's funny how people just relax when they hear what they want to hear. I guess the pain of struggle is too tough for most and they just let their guard down and trusted blindly after the civil rights bill was passed. That's just what "The D.E.A.D" planned on. This created a huge problem because as a nation of black folks, they never understood what freedom in the United States was. Really, how could they know about something they never had? The "D.E.A.D" knew this to be the case and exploited it for what would be their greater cause for self-preservation.

They continue today to exploit the uninformed, uneducated and faint-of-ear minorities. The number one tool was "money" followed by "fame".That dude Will my dad talked about was smart and beat them at their game and made millions. Now I understood why my pops wanted to be better, Willie walked in the light of what was going on and never in the dark. But Pops fell to the false feelings of fame that a dude gets from a woman when he has insecurities and now I am all alone they divorced. Funny things happen when two heads of a household part. I always looked at how happy mom made pops and that guided my preference for what a wife would look like more than anything else. I no longer had examples.

"When you talk about a revolution, most people think violence, violence, without realizing that the real content of any kind of revolutionary thrust lies in the principles and the goals that you're striving for not in the way you reach them."

— ANGELA DAVIS

Mom was in the crib by herself now. That's a picture of our crib above. Mamma's friend Anne was the first black woman I was ever afraid of. Then she became my testosterone-driven male role model. She did things in real life that I only saw on TV. She would always say, "For Angela." It wasn't till my second year in college that I understood she was talking about Angela Davis but now I know that was her role model.

Now, she was not easy on the eyes but was not ugly either. She had two sons around my age called Peanut and Fester. One day I remember seeing someone in a police uniform come to her house. Now at that age, anyone with a uniform on was the police and Pops had one that was similar so I stared out the window just hoping it was him. After what seemed to be half the day they came out one white and one black like on "Sanford and Son", then they just left no action at all; they just left. But then out came Anne, with a bat in her hand. My mom was standing by her just shaking her head. I was thinking oh shit she's bout to knock my mamma upside the head so I quickly ran outside all 3 feet 50 pounds of me. I thought I was bad because Anne started moving away from my mamma really fast. Yeah like it was me she was running from. I was still scared, though, because she was yelling, " Bitch I'm gonna fuck you up" By that time, I am next to my momma and she yells "Sally run". Now Sally was the only white lady that lived on the street. She loaned my mother her car sometimes, so mom looked out for her. Momma said she felt sorry for her because she almost got burned up cooking so now all she eats is baby food. Anyhow she had pissed off the big dawg of the Potomac Ave and it was on. Before Anne could get on Sally's porch, the police were back but Anne did not back down to them either.

This was the first time I saw a "North American" stand up to the police. Before this, I thought whatever the police said we had to do. But after today that will never be the same. Anne was like "fuck yawl that hippy bitch ain't out here saying I did anything pigs". She hates Yawl more than me. Now, "pig" was the term they used for the police. This went on for about ten minutes then everyone went their own way. Later, that night I overheard my mom talking about it. Now, Sally had loaned Anne the car and then said it was stolen. See Sally was supposed to go with her friend this thing called the Mayday Tribe but couldn't go because she didn't have a ride. They were going to shut the government down or something. I learned later on in college that this Mayday thing was about shutting down the government by marching in Washington. But what I learned that day was that I could stand up and stand up to anything that I knew was wrong. Now a beast is born. This was still too much for that era and at the end of the day the white landlords put their foot down and Anne had to move. Not long after Anne moved Mom was feeling the same way. It wouldn't be long before we had to go as well.

DEXTER & SONS
BARBER SHOP
MEN WOMEN & CHILDREN CUTS
12833
IES

BYE EAST CLEVELAND

As you could imagine, after the divorce, the ongoing Potomac Ave war between Anne and Sally, along with a son who tried to kill a kid when he was only in the first grade, my mom needed a change. So she went to the smartest and closest loved one she knew. It was the man himself, my "Uncle Buddy". I like to think of him as the prince of East Cleveland and I thought he was larger than life. He had even been to war and was back. My uncle used his GI Bill to purchase an apartment building down the street from his business, "Dexters Barbershop." The most impressive thing was his black Playboy bunny card. Man, the things kids find impressive out of ignorance unbelievable and I was impressed by my uncle.

Now, East Cleveland became primarily "North American" very quickly in the 1960s when the "North American" residents of Cleveland's East Side began to spread. It is wedged between the Italian community of Little Italy, the Irish community of Collinwood and the Jewish Communities of University and Cleveland Hts. With all the hatred going on, large groups of "North American" families looked for familiar surroundings and stayed together by relocating to East Cleveland, and my mom was looking to do the same. In direct line of what the opposers of the civil rights movement were saying, Niggers would do almost anything to think they were equal to whites and would literally try to emulate white folks. Thus, living in a big house that most called a mansion back in the day was like saying I made it. But under their blind eye caused by ignorance, most "North Americans" didn't get that renting the big house meant that white dude still owned it, and you had to answer to him as white flight was the way to go.

The ignorance of this mistake ultimately became the foundation of the fall of East Cleveland as we know it today. My uncle on the other hand, owned a six-suite apartment building and just happened to have a vacancy for his sister. Had the coolest barbershop in town. Dexter and Sons Barber Shop, photographed in May 2015. (Photo Above: Melanie Eversley, USA TODAY) This shop was home to many, including local entertainers who made it in the national spotlight, East Cleveland, baseball and softball teams, and both adults and children. Team Marathon, a mostly black running team that staged group runs through the city's hardscrabble streets, and if you were a black runner from Akron to Cleveland, no matter the age, this is where you came to be the best.

So, here we were for the first time in a place without Pops. I was now the man of the house and had no one to show me what that was. Ok, so let's just pause for a moment. What does this deck of cards look like? Is this a recipe for disaster or a recipe for success? Young boy in the early 70s, no father, single mother with no education who has four mouths to feed just seven (7) years removed from the civil rights movement. Let's get a full view of Mom. She is a pretty "North American" woman as best we know, the middle child of eight(8) siblings of one mother who had four(4) baby daddies out of Bessemer, Alabama and a father who was rumored to be a distant uncle that needed a young one in his household. Yeah, similar to that guy in "The Color Purple."

Time for school, East Cleveland Superior Elementary School second grade and just a lot of wide-eyed teachers talking about a lot of crazy adult stuff. Terrorists had just jacked up the Summer Olympics. The Vietnam War Ended, while the premier of the movie "The Godfather" had all of Little Italy ready to kill folks who came up Murray Hill., which was next door to East Cleveland. This thing called "Watergate" started when Mohamed Ali beat Floyd Patterson again, and the only thing I can remember for years was that it was ok for me to eat other people. Yeah, I was being taught by the media that to cook and eat another human was the way to go. Learned that in the second grade, following what was accepted in the world as smart. See, that year, some people crashed into a plane and ate their dead till they were rescued, and one of those was like this dark-skinned woman. So us Nigger (black) animals were cleared to eat other people. This made me pause and ask myself, am I being set up again by "The D.E.A.D" was all I kept asking myself. Then, all I could do was shut that teacher off. I just didn't listen to a word she had to say anymore. Somehow, that same ghost that was saving me from those things in the closet and under my bed just told me to shut her down.

Now, her replacement was what I would like to call my saving grace... Now, do not get this thing twisted. No one replaced her for class. I just found another teacher that got my attention, and as our gang says, "And how?". Till today, I can't remember her name, but she had me feeling a funny kind of way. Actually, she was all I could hear when I was in her class. I even got mad when other dudes would have conversations with her. I was the only one who was supposed to get that time. Looking back on it now, and with all the wood I had in her class, I know that was my first crush.

Because I wanted her time, I had to figure out how to get in those conversations that were going on... I got bits and pieces, and it was as if she had a boyfriend named Kelly who played something called football. She just loved Kelly. I had no idea what football was, but I needed to know and was blinded from learning anything in school till I could get in on this conversation. Plus, how did the other boys know him? I knew I was missing something, and yep, it was a Pops, but I think I got this one on my own. One day, I just stayed close to the desk just to listen and I heard her say Larry Kelly should have got the ball to one of the boys. The boy said no, they should have thrown it. Now, I didn't really know what they were talking about, but I could tell she didn't like what he said, so I took up for my lady and was like, "Dude, you wrong. Larry is the best player." Now, they both paused, looked at me and at the same time said, "What". Now, I can't back down, so I repeated it: "Larry is the best player." The boys started to just laugh at me while she looked away, shaking her head.

After lunch, I was sitting in my seat and still had some gum in my mouth. Back then, that was like smoking a joint in class. She saw me and called me out on it. Man, I was having a fucked up day. Now, in those days, class discipline was left to the teacher, and this was the pre-child abuse days, and they kept their own piece of wood just hanging on the wall. She called me up to the board and said the magic words, "That's three touches of rail" Shit, she was for real. She swung the light on the first one while saying, "That's for the gum." The second one was a little softer:" That's for the Browns." That caught me off guard, and I looked up at her, but the third one was on the way from behind her head bam '" that was for Leroy Kelly." Oh, my ass was stinging while my eyes were popping out of my head, and my feelings were like you dumbass, you said the wrong name. The rest of the week was like a blur. I was caught between listening to a teacher who wanted me to eat other people and not being able to hear from a teacher because she didn't think I was human.

Over the weekend, my mom had a friend named Robert Gay. He was a big man, much like my Pops, so I thought I would give him a shot. In the past, I didn't spend much time around him, but this weekend, he brought his son with him. The kid's name was Dean. He seemed a little slow, you know, like what they called retards during that era. They were in the front room watching TV, so I said if Dean can watch TV with him so can I. It was some type of game on a field. It looked really confusing, but Rob was into it. Then I heard him say go Csonka, and I could tell he was talking about the guy on the TV. The more he talked, the more I began to figure out what was going on. Then it was done, and I heard the magical words, "Larry Csonka ran all over them Steelers." I get it ahh Larry was the bad guy, and that's my name. I just laughed. The next day, out of spite of the other dudes and to stroke this newly formed ego, I said to one of the boys, "Csonka. Larry Csonka like me." I said it just loud enough for her to hear. From that day forward, I had an identity that I was defending, one that was modeled after a hero that I might be able to emulate. The next weekend Rob did not come over, but I made sure I found the station that played the game. However, that task started a chain reaction of shit that would affect the relationship with me and my family for the rest of my life.

VIOLENCE OF GENERATION X

Latch key kids we became. The question is was this planned or just happen by chance? Well, let's first look at its foundation. If someone is home ya can't be a latchkey kid. If mom and dad are part of the family, ya can't be a latchkey kid. If the community works together as one big family, ya can't be a latchkey kid. Ok, I got my answer, shit I've been set up. The revolutionaries lost and temptation got mom and pops. Shit I am a latchkey kid, malnutrition and all, but more than that, I am "Generation X" The middle child of the 70s. We "Generation X" children were seen as mediocre on the family's big scale. The older child was clearly annoyed by the middle child because he felt there was a huge intelligence difference. This leads the way to the older one being the cool one. The younger kids got the attention at high levels for nothing more than the natural origins of nurturing. But Gen X had to fend for themselves. Disappointments were a regular occurrence. Damn you President Lyndon B. Johnson that addressed a joint session of Congress, on On March 15, saying, "There is no issue of states' rights or national rights. There is only the struggle for human rights." Yeah, you knew we had already waited 100 years, and the time for waiting was no more.

Now, "the trap" was this new thing I learned from my granddaddy and in its simplest terms means giving your freedoms away by your actions. Well, my actions were picking at the cheese like a hungry mouse. Violence became my number one picking tool.

After I got to watch the 1972 Super Bowl I was geeked up. One of the stimuli came from an unlikely source and that was that fight I had with my big sister. I, the middle, unintelligent, uncool kid won the fight and got what he wanted. What a fucked up recipe. From that day forward anytime she got in the way we went at it. Then it got even worse. I found myself sitting on the floor at the foot of my mom's bed at night watching Bo Bo Brazil. He was teaching me moves that I could use. Bo Bo was the top "All American" wrestler of that day. He was known for the coco butt. He would knock cats out just by pounding his hard forehead on his opponent's head. It was quick, it was vicious and I used it on her. What a move! Now, most of our fights were over food. How silly that sounds. But back in the day when the only people home to make sure we ate was us, that's how it went down. Then a second component kicks in. She gets help. You ever heard the term, "snitches get stitches"? Well, that was the next round. She started to tell and I began to get a series of beatings from my mother like you wouldn't believe. Shit we were all caught in the "trap" now. Under today's laws mamma would have been arrested just because of the extension cord whelps on my legs and back. Sometimes I couldn't tell which lasted longer the extension cord or the switch tree whelps.

I think my momma thought I hated my sister. But it was actually the total opposite. I loved my sister. I really was a "Generation X" kid and thought she was smart. She knew more than me because she was in the fourth grade. But my ego did take a boost whooping on that fourth graders and from then on I never saw age or grade as a factor for dudes or girls. This opened the doors for me to be fearless about venturing away from home. Now, like I said I really did love my sister and every time I hurt her I really did feel bad. However, every time I would get beat for hurting her I would quickly forget and fault her for my pain. So, to avoid the whole thing I just stopped coming home. Here comes the "trap."

Where does a six-year-old go instead of home after school? It's easy, the streets, just wandering from a friend's house to a friend's house. Then nature kicks in. The grum-bellies kicked in like you wouldn't believe. So you figure it out. Where would a six-year-old kid go to get his belly full instead of home? The blind eye was at work, but I had to eat. The only likely place was the store. Yeah, you know, because most of you have done it too. My fingers got real sticky and "Three Musketeers" were my favorite mark. You got it right by the age of six I was a real good thief, I had to eat. Now, nutrition was not the issue, just something to eat. The better I got it, the longer I stayed away from home. I got so good at it that I now had stashes of candy. Then it happened. I get home, go to my stash and it's gone. Ok, here comes the "Trap." Off the rip anger kicks in and it has already been trained to focus on my sister. So, I take a B-line straight for her. Now, unbeknownst to me, mamma was home and she cut me off. Now, this was a first and caught me off guard. Then I saw it. My "Three Musketeers'" in her hand. All the thievery gave me a sense of confidence. I had become pretty savvy; and before she could say anything I just asked the question, "was that one of mine?" But something was still odd, no one else was around. They were home but were locked in the room. Now, I was a runner at that age, meaning I did not stand still for beating. It was a workout and probably what made me so slippery on the football field years later. But on this day I wasn't in the mood so I got out in front of the problem. "Hey, ma I been going up to granddad doing work, he said hi." He gave me some change for helping him, so I got some candy. That lie slid out my mouth so fast. I used to think the devil put those words in my mouth just because.

Now, my granddaddy was a real stern God, fearing church-loving deacon and mom did not spend a lot of time over there. They were one of the first black East Cleveland homeowners and lived on the next block over. He was big on church, Mt. Nebo Baptist and he insisted that Mamma and her sister attend. They were grown now and had their own direction of life but he was still king of the family even though he was not their father. The thought of me being around him sort of helped her out with him. But, this was my first lie to my mamma. Of all the bad things I had done up to that point for some reason, I had never lied to my mamma.

The next day like a brave kid walking into a haunted house I went to my grandparents' house and volunteered to do work around the house. It was actually cool and I spent all my spare time there. Oh man, something was keeping the "Trap" from locking me in. I couldn't believe it, momma was cautious about beating me, and I had stopped fighting with my sister. There was no need to have sticky fingers anymore as Mimmi and Granddad gave me all the ice cream I wanted, and I was no longer in the cold streets after school with spring being on the horizon. Most of all I had a male who cared about me and was again in my life.

ARSON

James Dexter was the man I knew as my granddaddy. He was the reigning matriarch of the family. Some would say he was a frightening man who wore an Adolf Hitler mustache. It did not matter to me because he was the reason I had no more beatings. It was strange as I was the one in the family who visited. He kept two rather large German Shepherds behind a hogans hero fence. Not even my grandmother dared to get near the dogs. But he made sure they got along with me. From adult to child I was the only one who appeared to not be afraid to be around him and that made me feel special. He was the opposite of my Pops' side of the family though. It was like MLK (grandaddy) and Malcolm X (Pops' side of the family).

I had an uncle, lord bless his sole uncle Alvin, who was a bank robber. He literally would take a gun, go into the neighborhood bank, hold them at gunpoint and take money. Till today we still wonder if any money is hidden in the walls of grandad's house. J.D. then introduced me to the "trap" as he knew it. It is still so clear, just me, him and the two German shepherds on the back porch. Them eating Hough Bakery bread and me homemade ice cream. He said two things to me. The first was, "I don't have to go to jail. Never, let anyone let you believe that it's ok to go to jail and that this happens to everyone and it's just your turn. You do not have to go. The "trap" is you letting them steal that away from you."

Now, I am just a six-year-old kid with a simple mind so I asked who the honkeys? Thinking, when black folks start talking about somebody doing something to them it's always white folks. He surprised me and I think that's why I still remember it. He said "No". It is plum thinking and to be plum is to be right. The right thing is the most difficult thing for a human being to possess. It is desired by individuals and groups as they want people to believe they are right which equals them being intellectual". I stopped him and asked, "What's that? He said, "How do smart people want other people to think they are." He went on, "Ok, You want friends right? And you want them to like you and think you know stuff that they should? I replied "Yep". "Well son that's being intellectual, "I said, " I can't say it but I get it." I was thinking that's sort of what I did to mom. He went on "the actual physical acts that comprise of "right" is by far the hardest task humans are faced with and are often stolen. I stopped him again, "I don't get that". It was cool because he seemed to like me stopping him when I didn't get it. He went on to explain that we can't just be here, we are going to do something and even if it's wrong we are doing it because we think it's right by us personally and we just got to do it." I said ok, "like fighting somebody that broke into the house." Yes, it's wrong to fight but right in that situation. But sometimes people trick you into thinking the situation is the right one, now they are stealing this physical act from you and you have to be punished. When you get punished they will write it down and tell the whole world to go read it. and be warned that you would hurt them. After that, peoplet y won't treat you the way they treat those they believe won't hurt them. They put you in a group and tell the world to fear that group." I stopped him and asked what group they put him in? He told me that's why I said you don't have to go to jail, you can pick your own group. I picked my group and I am a "Mason" that means I am plum and when you become a man if given a chance become a mason become a mason. Today, I have a square tip burn mark across my left breast because of that lesson.

The shepherds, both the lads and the lasses, did what comes naturally, and before long, there were pups running about! I was over the moon, just couldn't help myself—caught up in the joy of watching them grow. J.D. started giving them away, and then there was just one little fella left. He put a beaming smile on my face when he handed him to me. I was floating, just like a dream. I promised to take care of him. I bolted home with this little creature, and my mum, well, she finally saw how much time I was spending in that old place. We created a cozy nook for him down in the basement. I covered everything with newspaper, set his bowl filled with water and puppy chow like a little prince. But it wasn't just us in my uncle's flat; there were a handful of other families as well. As a six-year-old kid, I was blissfully unaware of the fuss my pup was making. But they sure took notice, and it wasn't a good kind of attention. You remember the snitches, right? They started complaining to my uncle, saying the pup was making too much racket during the night. I suppose he missed me and his mum and would whimper a bit. But they had to make it sound like a full-blown rock concert. So one day, after school, I came home to find my little buddy gone. Just like that, poof! My uncle had given him away—no questions asked, no apologies, just vanished. I wasn't heartbroken, but there was a void. The shame, the embarrassment regarding that pup was too much; I didn't want to face J.D. and lie to him about my failure. So, visiting there was suddenly out of the question.

And there I was again, wondering, feeling that familiar "trap" creeping back in.

I am pissed. I am hooked on not going home worse than heroin addicts of that day. Now, my uncle Buddy was still a cool cat and he had the finest women. I thought he had two women, Pearl and Michelle. No disrespect intended, I actually thought they were like Playboy Bunnies. Anyhow, because of his lifestyle he was never home and just happened to live in the apartment just under us. He was never home and with women like that, I wouldn't be home either. The old homes back then had jacked-up locks that's probably why break-ins were happening all the time. Well as you could guess, I figured out how to get into the back door. Man I done found me a new hideout. Now, of course, I went through his stuff, who wouldn't? I don't remember much but I do remember his Playboy Bunny membership card. It was black with gold writing and a gold Playboy bunny emblem with his name Robert Dexter. Yeah, now you see why I thought his girl was a Playboy bunny. He did keep some food in the fridge but not much.

One day I was real hungry and remembered seeing some cookie dough in his fridge. I get the dough, taste it. and spit it out. That's how dumb I was. I remembered a TV commercial that showed cookies being made in this "Easy Bake Oven " so the light went on, AHHH... Now, for some reason, the stove was not on. I now know he was shackin' with Michelle and nothing was on. I had to make these cookies. Those old apartments all came with fireplaces that the x-mas tree went by. AHHH light on again bright idea. Let's just use the fireplace. So, I found some newspaper, some matches and lit that sucker up. Man, this is cool, I wonder how big this fire can get... I was so fascinated with the fire that I forgot about the cookies.. Now, those old homes were full of wood, including the floor. What my dumbass didn't know was that those were fake fireplaces made for gas of some sort and that the base was wood. I done set the fire on the ceramic and wood part and now it's getting big. Time to run. I quickly ran out the back door and upstairs. I am pacing, hoping for something I don't even know. Then it happens, it's here. A fire truck is coming down the street. Us latch key kids were just looking out the windows. Then folks outside watching started yelling "Get out get out" I knew what was going on and told everyone to follow me and we ran out the back and down the stairs.

Now, it was me against the two giants "Trap" and "Discretion". I knew everyone saw all of us together in the window but someone had to go down. Just across the street was another latchkey kid. Her name was Angie. She lives with only her dad and some cats. Her house was nasty and she was called a fast little girl for whatever that meant and most adults were, like, staying away from her. So, when I was asked if I saw anything the first thing that came out of my mouth was, "I saw Angie, I saw Angie come out of the building" Until the writing of this book, the only two people who knew I lied were me and her. Angela of Delmont Ave in East Cleveland Ohio I am so sorry. As you can imagine, after the divorce, the ongoing Potomac Ave war between Anne and Sally, along with a son who tried to kill a kid when he was only in the first grade, and set their apartment building on fire, my mom needed a change. Bye, East Cleveland, it was a wonderful run.

ITS MY FAULT, MAMMA

East Cleveland today with Euclid Avenue as its main thoroughfare looks like something out of a Planet of the Apes movie. Grass-overgrown lots appear between clusters of houses, many of which appear empty. Wildlife everywhere deer, possums, skunks even the occasional citizen riding horseback. There is still a resident or two watering grass or quietly sipping a soft drink on a porch as if defying the community's reputation for danger. Ok, back to the story.

It's summertime and mom had to get out of East Cleveland so she fell back on her go-too, Ann. Ann had moved to the projects in Cleveland on the 55th. The Outhwaite Housing Projects it was for us. Now, for those who know nothing about public housing, it's a mess but the folks that live there have no clue about that. Everyone just does the best that they can. We had a swimming pool, basketball courts, fields and the candy man. Now, we were more or less swatters. You had to apply to the government to get approved and they had limits. We just snuck in with Anne. There were nine of us in the small apartment. With nine folks in a tiny three-bedroom apartment, you know what I did. You might as well call me that orphaned son Caine from the show "Kung Fu"; because I was always looking for somewhere to walk and an adventure to get into. I think I kept moving to avoid capture by the "Trap." And what I had come to realize was that I had avoided the "Traps" and was more fortunate to see them.

This setup was perfect because it was this hole in the ground that was to keep people down. It would give just enough to not go desperate and small enough to not get ambitious. For the most part, the kids in the projects were happy and had daily things to look forward to. The number one thing was "The Candy Man". Now the projects didn't need a store; the store came to it. The parking lots were like road maps and they had streets connected to them instead of blocks. The candy man took the place of the ice cream truck. Penny candy it was. Now Later, Sweat Sours, Blow Pops, Mary Janes, Lemon Heads, Red Hots man you name it and all in the name of Pennies. If you ran around the neighborhood ringing his x-mas bell so that folks knew he was there he would give you free candy. My first paying job was right in front of my eyes.

I am seven now and it's time to make some money and I could care less if it's candy. By my second week in the projects I figured out his route. I really didn't know how to tell time but I could figure out when he was close to what was on TV. I called it "As the World Turns" When I heard the sound of that music it was time to get near the pool area and wait to take the bell like a track runner takes a baton in a relay race. There it is and here I go. Most kids would run around just enough to get one sucker and then give it back. Me on the other hand had nowhere to go so I just ran around and around while he was driving his truck. I got a real workout without even knowing it. We will talk about this a little later. What did happen though was I became the candy man's go-to guy because I ran not only through the streets but the buildings as well and this brought in more kids. It got to the point where I had more candy than I could eat just because I could run.

Now, the candy man didn't stay all day and then it happened. I became a true American. I was walking from the pool eating some candy and a kid asked me for some. I had more than enough so I pulled out my stash and gave him one. The next day there were three more kids with him all asking for candy. Now, this wasn't happening so I said I only had enough for one of yawl. Then a kid pulled out a quarter and asked to buy the one piece I had not eaten. Now, I got this candy for free. The candy man was selling them for pennies and I knew I had more so this was a no-brainer. I felt guilty though so I gave him three pieces, just enough for him and his friends. For the next two days, more kids would come to me at the pool asking for candy. They were calling the candy man my uncle and thought that's why I had so much candy and was always ringing the bell.

Then the worst thing that could happen happened, it rained. See when it rained the candy man didn't come. If the candy man didn't come then I got no candy to sell. It rained for three straight days. On that third night, all I kept thinking about was how to get more candy. I knew I had to stockpile my candy and need to ring that bell and buy some. I knew the cost and had some money but I was three cents short for what I wanted to buy. Now, Anne had this funny-looking bottle and in the bottom of it were pennies. Yep, I thought nothing of it and took out the three pennies and went on my way. I was back in business and for the next five or six days I was cleaning up.

Even though I had money to buy the candy, if I thought I needed a penny or two to buy more I would just take it out of the bottle. I remember watching something on TV about putting your money under the mattress so that's where I kept my bank and candy. One day, I get home and Anne is just sitting on the front steps. I say hi, go in the front door and she comes in right after me. I look over and all the kids are sitting on the couch. All six of them. She then said with Sally's voice `I'm gonna kick yawls ass voice, "I am only gonna ask yawl once. Who's been stealing my pennies?" She had the bottle in her hand and as I looked at it there were just a few left. I kept thinking I couldn't have taken all of those maybe someone else was jacking her too. Then she got a belt and made it do a popping sound. Now, for me, I really wasn't that scared after all she wasn't my mamma and I got geek up before to get at her when I thought she was going after my mamma when all the while she was going after Sally. My big sister on the other hand commenced singing like a canary, "I know where it's at, I know who did it, Junie did it. Junie did it." She then ran to the room with Anne following and lifted up the corner of the mattress exposing my safe with candy and money. Ok, by now you know me. A three-person fight started immediately. I don't know why but I could have cared less that Anne was standing right there so I started whooping her ass. One would have thought I had trained Ali and Frazier the way I was throwing my hands. While I was throwing mine and my sister throwing back Anne was trying to get at me because of the pennies and everyone else was crying and yelling. It was crazy. What's funny though is it all seemed like slow motion to me and the crazier it got the safer I felt about really being in trouble. Somehow it all ended, it ended for everyone but me.

Later that night mamma comes home, yeah with no words, not even an explanation I got that extension cord beating. Throughout the whole time, she just told me "Don't open your mouth, don't open your mouth." That whole night I was so mad that I didn't really feel the pain from the whelps, I just kept thinking about how they all missed the point. See, Anne had a bottle of pennies and pennies were missing, I had a mattress full of quarters, nickels and dimes, sprinkled with some candy. I was the one who just got robbed. Nonetheless, I was a thief and we had to go. Sorry, yawl I did it again. Now, your brother and son, the attempted murderer, arson, and thief have taken away your home again. Where to now? The answer is phase one of Desegregation.

AN ACTIVIST IS BORN

Do you ever get the feeling that folks know you did something even though they are not saying anything? Well, I think the grown-ups knew I had something to do with the fire and it put a lot on the shoulders of my mom. She was actually just like me or me just like her and I now know she did whatever she needed to do for her babies. So, for the first time we left town out on our own. There was no crutch, to lean on we just left everyone behind and headed to the boogie town, of Dayton, Ohio. Now, I did have an aunt there but mom was determined to do this one on her own. Shit, I didn't see any family from Cleveland for about four years to include pops. It was the bicentennial year 1976 red, white and blue the next time I saw anyone. I had begun the process of being set free. The fuel, unknown to me at that time, was Desegregation.

Dayton fits the typical image of a Midwestern former industrial center for workers Historically it was a place where racial segregation had persisted despite many efforts for change. Thus, the desegregation order of Dayton schools was significant to the future of North American families and those who knew this hit it with everything they had., Dayton and its suburbs were found to be the third most racially segregated communities among the fifty largest metropolitan areas in the United States. The only metropolitan area in the state with higher levels of racial segregation than Dayton was Cleveland, and I just landed right smack in the middle of things starting at Wogaman Elementary School.

I am the new kid on the block, third grade smart group. Man was that class fucked up. I had this white teacher who dressed up every day like she was on "Little House on the Prairie" Because I was the new kid on the block I got to sit with who I thought were the cool kids. Then it happened. First, let me say I have been good since we made the move. I couldn't remember the last time I had hit my sister. I was the man of the family and had to do better. I remembered how it felt when I asked questions when JD was talking to me so this is what I did in class. If it felt good then it should feel good now. So one day I was working on a math worksheet and I just didn't understand. This is the third grade and we were only doing multiplication and division but I just couldn't understand the long version of division. I really needed to get the concept of why I put a certain number in certain places so I asked that question. Little House on the Prairie lady came along and said, "I told you, is something wrong with you" then she proceeded to talk to the class about division then asked me for the answer to one of the questions and I answered I don't know. She came over to me and asked me again this time pointing at the number on my sheet and stated, "What makes sense".

Again, I don't understand. Then this fool grabbed me. She had the nerve to actually grab me. Then she said clear as day in front of everyone. I'm putting you with the retarded group. Now, there was another set of kids that was on the other side of the room. She released my shirt once she guided me over there. I just sat, trying to figure out what just happened. Then she handed me a sheet that started with 1+1=, 2+1=, 3+1= and so on all the way to 100. I stayed in the group doing preschool math for the rest of the year.

Over that summer we moved to a cool neighborhood with a basketball court out back, free lunch in the park and new furniture. Mamma had a new gig at Concord City department store and we started to get a change of clothes and shoes. The shoes were what I liked the best because I always wore my jeepers till they had a hole in the bottom. Hey, I had something on my feet and that was all that mattered. But having a new pair of shoes for a change and two TVs in the house made it feel like we were rich and I was the man of the house. We really had not ever lived as good as we were living, and it felt like we were, well, special.

When the school year started I was full of anxiety, I stopped at the IGA market across from Wogaman to get some candy before school then rolled on across the parking lot just high on life. When I got to my classroom there she was Little Miss House on the Prairie. Shit, why is she following me. She was my teacher again. Man, my morale dropped so quickly I thought I was in "Charlie Brown's" classroom just hearing wa wa wa, wa wa wa. In those days the teacher would escort her class to its specials and she was taking us to art. I was happy because I could at the least be away from her. I guess not being happy becomes an opening for the D.E.A.D.s "Trap", because halfway down the stairs this thing from the year 1875 decides to put her hands on me again, trying to shuffle me along. Now, all summer I thought about what she did the last time. I was getting that defensive feeling sort of like how I was feeling when the boys in the first grade were talking about my mamma. I had promised myself before I tried to stab them that if they stayed cool all would be cool but if they didn't all hell gonna break loose. Well in my mind she was placed in the same little bottle as they were and it had been fermenting the whole summer. Before I knew it I had bitch slapped the lady like they did women in the movie " Superfly". right there on the stairway. It was just one slap then a two-hand shove, "Bitch don't put your hands on me." Everyone started running away from us like we had the plague. That goes to show how times change. Today everyone would have run to us with cell phones in hand in full video mode. Anyway from what I can remember after that, there was no suspension, mamma was told and I was placed in a totally new classroom with an "All American" teacher. Is this what you get for standing up to institutionalized racist?

My new teacher was a sister who looked out for me. I was back with the smart group and when she saw my work she got pissed about them saying I was a retard. She had the music teacher work with me as she said the band would give me a way to express myself. I tried but the music teacher suggested the clarinet and we couldn't afford the clarinet. That was the instrument that was best for my crooked teeth, he said. I was able to get on the school patrol guards to help the students cross the street and was in charge of the long yellow poles with stop signs. I even had the orange Hitler shoulder belt and a police badge. The most enriching thing that she did though was give me a lead in the school play about American Indians. They all seemed so utterly surprised that I could say my part without looking at my paper. It was like I was "Doogie Howser" or something. She kept bringing people to hear me say my part as if to say I told you so. Then she gave me a letter to give to my mom. It said I would represent the school at an assembly at the school board performing my part of the play. I still remember that day I had on a new blue Indian print shirt and dress pants and it was only me and ma. What they didn't know was that it was nothing, I had done it a thousand times in the basement of Mt. Nebo Baptist Church in East

Cleveland. See although we didn't go to church every Sunday we did go to church every Easter and all the kids had to be in the Easter program to get a meal. So every year we had to learn your part of the play and we wanted to laugh at the person who forgot what to say and I didn't like being laughed at. That was my last year at Wogaman.

Today I understand the pressure that was there. It was a war zone created by people's resistance to desegregation and I did not realize that at that time. The blacks and whites were being forced to be together, especially as workers. We were despised by our white teachers. Not all but enough. Our "North American" teachers were faced with the task of proving them wrong. Then here came the perfect combination of a teacher who cared and a student willing. The two of us together showed them we are no different, so please rewind and change your values. This change is not just for me but for you as well so you can live your life knowing the truth. The Activist was now born.

MRS. PEARL

As the shadows deepened, life took on an unsettling air, a spectral dance of fate unraveling before me. It seemed as though souls were conjured forth, summoned to prepare me for an unseen battle—a grim struggle for the sake of others bound in concerns not yet understood. Threads of existence wove together in a tapestry of sorrow; my dear mother, distant and solitary, stood encumbered by the weight of her progeny. In the relentless grasp of labor, my siblings and I found ourselves marooned in the echoing silence of abandoned hours. Thus emerged our first formidable guardian, a creature of steadfast presence—Miss Pearl, a name I shall etch eternally in the recesses of my memory. She, with her singular daughter, bore the burden of two rascally nephews, Tyrone and Lester, who now assumed the mantle of elder siblings in our youthful realm of innocence. In those times, the once-vibrant city of Dayton teemed with the fervor of athletic prowess, a veritable cauldron where the very essence of sport thrummed with life. Amongst the passions ignited, it was the sport of football that rose to the pinnacle, a calling to which many were compelled to answer, and thus, I, too, found myself drawn forth in this grand pursuit of glory.

Now, I had gotten a little taste of what it felt like to be the go-to guy playing football right before we left the projects in Cleveland and, I mean, right before. The week before we left I was watching some older kids playing in the field by the swimming pool. I was too embarrassed about the stealing thing to go swimming with everyone else in the house, so I just stayed outside the building. Then it happened, they called over, "Hey, candy man, you wanna play?" I just hunched my shoulders and ran over. Ok, what you need? He told me to just block for him. I was like, "What's that?" He then pointed to a guy and said, "Just get in his way when I run." I'm thinking, shit, that's cool. A guy snapped the ball and he started to run so I started to run but the ball hit me. I guess I got in the way. They all yelled. pick it up," I did, and then they said, "run, run, man." So I took off, scared to death, more about them getting mad at me than anything else. Then it happened, someone grabbed me, and those reflexes I had developed from all the fighting with my sister and running from whoopings kicked in and I just shook him off. By that time, another cat was trying to get me. I shook him off, too, and everyone said ahhh. That ahhh sounded so good I wanted to hear it again. Before you knew it, I had scored. The next time we got the ball, the dude explained to me that he would get the ball first, then hand it to me and for me to just follow him. Here we go, and yep, you can guess what happened. I took it to the house. They were either too weak or too slow to stop me. The next couple of days, they would come to our apartment to pick me up so that I could play with them. So when it was time to leave for Dayton that was what I missed the most, those ahhhs.

Now, I had a chance to get 'em again. The difference here, though, is we were not on a field. It was the hard concrete street. Now, unlike the first time in Cleveland, I was on defense first. Tyrone snapped the ball, Bobby, and instead of running it, these dudes like to throw. There were these brothers, the Wooden brothers, that lived on the corner and Bobby, who was the best athlete on the street, threw it to one of those Wooten boys. I can't remember which one but what I do remember is that he caught the ball and was running right at me. So you know what I did. Smack, I caught him clean, with me running full speed, both his feet went up in the air, then the ball was in the air, we both landed somewhere between the curb and some bushes. Not only did I get some aahhs but some OOOOSss as well. Then all the boys were telling me, "We not playing tackle. We not playing tackle." I said, "I know it's football" Lester goes, "Knawl man, its touch, just touch him." Mrs. Pearl was watching the whole thing and came running to make sure that kid was alright. Well, that ended the game for that day, but we played almost every day, two to three times a day. It was good. We actually got so good we would go to other blocks and neighborhoods just to play and show them who was the best. If there was a Lombardi trophy for street football we would have been the Super Bowl Champs.

Now that I look back on it, Mrs. Pearl was really watching over the whole street. When it would get dark, all the kids would just hang out with us in the driveway, back yard or sun porch if it was raining. Her house was the park. But once it got dark and it was time for everyone to go in. For the first time in my life there was a woman teaching me about life. Up to this point in life, I only had two people try to tell me about the dangers I would have to look out for as I lived in this world. The other two were James Dexter and Pops.

The year was 1976 and I can remember it like it was yesterday because Mrs. Pearl made sure we all sat down and watched the Olympics. There was a local kid running that year and she would tell us he was a role model that we should follow. He was Dayton's hero of the 1976 Olympics. Now, I had no idea what the Olympics were, but somehow, knowing that someone she knew was in it made me really tune in. He was a hurdler. Edwin Moses was his name. I followed him round after round. I would count how many steps he would take as he went around the track. I thought that was what it was about.

Then on the last day for the hurdles all the kids came in to watch. I really thought I was the only one that was interested in being like him. After all I was the athlete around here that was getting ahhhs and ooos. It wasn't till that night that I realized he was running to be the best in the world. That you get a gold coin worth millions just for being first. Runners set, pop, the gun went off and Moses shot out the starting blocks. He normally attacked that first hurdle. He wore glasses, his number was 943 and he was in lane four(4) so I knew that was him, but he was behind. I can close my eyes today and still see it. I can even remember the guy on TV saying, "Let's see if the people in Dayton, Ohio, will be able to cheer for Edwin the champion." or something like that. Then I lost count because it was like he took 9 steps instead of 12 on the third hurdles, then he was back in 12 steps by the fourth hurdles and I yelled, "he just won yawl, he just got that gold." Everyone looked at me like I was crazy. Someone even said the race was not over. Well, if you were looking at TV, it was. He was just approaching the second curve, but if you knew Moses you knew it was done, like the answer to the Nike swoosh, DONE. I will forever remember his time. You see, the best lane on the track is 4. His lane, the world's lucky number, is 7, and well, God brought me into this world 6-5-65. Edwin had just set the world record with a time of 47.65. It was fate.

Everyone else was so excited they actually ran out of the house and into the streets. Neighbors were shouting, pleased with the results. But I found myself stuck on the TV, I saw something I thought was real strange. For the first time, I saw a black person and a white person hugging each other. Then they held hands and even raised them in the air. I looked over my shoulder and noticed Mrs. Pearl watching me. She then asked me if I was alright. I just shrugged my shoulders and pointed to the TV at Edwin and the White guy who was holding his hand as they ran around the track. She knew I was puzzled. She then went on to explain that this was more than just a race. We have a lot of problems here, especially where Edwin's mother works. She is part of the schools, and a lot of people don't think that blacks and whites can be together, and that's what they want to do with the schools. I then went on to tell her about what happened to me with the Little House on the Prairie teacher. She then validated the feeling I was getting. She assured me folks were working to make things better between the races, especially Edwin's grandmother, who was on the school board. People are really talking bad about his grandmother but she is the one who will help people to know it's ok; Edwin's actions just prove she is right. What he is doing is just showing everyone it's ok. Man, Edwins and his entire family were right in the middle of Desegregation and the "D.E.A.D" fight to keep the reins of power.

From then on, Mrs. Pearl always made it a point to explain things to me that involved social conscious issues and I thank her for that. I had a chance to meet Edwin each summer over the next two years as I would compete in the track and field event for youths at the University of Dayton. He loved giving back, teaching, giving tips, and today, the street that is named after him is right next to the first track I ever ran on. He became the foundation of my track & field coaching philosophies that I continue to win championships with today. Oh, I forgot Edwin got even luckier. They dropped his record time by putting his lane number at the end, so instead of 47.65, its 47.64.

Although our communities had been attacked with sex, drugs, malt liqueur, prostitution, porn and money. That spirit that has allowed Africans to survive since the beginning of man was alive and hard at work. That was evident with Edwin. Paths were also being cleared that folks didn't even know they would travel. This was the bicentennial year and fireworks were the call of the day, especially in Cleveland. The greed over sex, drugs, malt liquor and money was pouring into those communities adjacent to East Cleveland. I could hear Rob and my mamma talking about it being a war zone with real bombings, especially the Irish, week after week after week. I even saw it on the news one evening at Mrs. Pearl's house; someone was trying to bomb the Irishman. Then I was thinking, I am glad I am not there. But now I know things were just getting cleaned up. Oh, yea, Rob did make that occasional visit all the way to Dayton. It was cool with me if it made mamma happy.

THE TOWNVIEW "OUR GANG"....

Dayton was really treating my mother better than Cleveland. She was working, her kids appeared to be ok. We had even moved into a home for the first time in a community called Townview. Just living in a house makes you feel rich. Especially this one because it had a swimming pool in the backyard. It didn't work but we had a pool. A new house, 5225 Rucks Rd., which meant a new school. (Picture above) A new house meant a new school and Townview Elementary it was. This is where I met my friends for life. But it started off kind of rough. There was Mike Jones, Clarence McGill, Darren Champ and Daryl Hill. All of us were in Mrs. Cook's classes. She was a nice looking teacher who had a cool husband with a perfect afro.

For the first time, I just let my guard down and accepted them as friends. During those days, we had recess and they like most kids of that day the boys liked to play football. Yep, it was that time again, but this time I just did my offensive thing and scored as much as I could. Funny thing was, all of them were already playing on like a real professional team with helmets and shoulder pads. They all played for the Rams.

Every Monday they would come to school talking about the game and how they won. Then we would go out for recess and I would be the one getting the ahhhh moment. In a matter of time the obvious happened. They were like we could use you on our team. Now, they didn't know I was looking for them every Sunday on TV, all the time but never saw them so I began to think it was just a joke and they were making fun of me.

Then they caught me on a bad day. It was one of those days when I half-heard something. While at lunch, they were like Daryl said he wanted to fight. I quickly answered, "Yawl know I will kick his ass." Then some girl was like, I'm gonna go tell him. I was real quick to yell, "So." Now, with this modern-day "our gang" group of ours, Daryl was the little one and why he wanted the ass-kicking, I couldn't imagine. But if that's what he wants, then I'm gonna give it to him. Before school ended, these fools had set it up better than Don King himself. The stage was at the side of the school by the cornfield. When I got there, it seemed like half the school was there. I walked up, and here comes this dude I had never seen before, "So you want to kick my ass." I looked at Mike and was like, " Who is that?" He replied, "You know Daryl." Shit, I did pick a fight with the wrong Daryl, and it was too late to back down. He was having an issue with the new guy at the school, me, and was marking his territory. Oh, well, I am in it now. He then bailed me out while signing his death penalty. "Fuck you and yo black ass mamma too," he yelled. For me, talking about my mamma was like feeding spinach to Popeye. He was trying to box, yea right, I thought. So I threw a couple of punches, then said what the hell and went into wrestling mode. Slammed the dude to the ground, then went into boxing mode. Before I knew it, everyone was running away, and me and him were left there with teachers pulling us apart.

What I did not know was that the courts had mixed the

"North Americans" with a really bad group of the "D.E.A.D." in a community called Trotwood Madison and called it desegregation. Me and Daryl were acting just like those who opposed integrating blacks and whites said we would. Because of this, I was taken home. Before the next day of school, my mamma knew I had been in a fight. Now beating my ass at that age was a little different, I would, on reflex, take that manly posture, but I knew better and would just submit. But while submitting I tried I really tried to tell her they were talking about her, but she was not having it. For peace of mind, she said we would be going back to Mrs. Pearl's House on weekends or when she could; I guess she felt it was safer that way. For me, I couldn't wait to get back to school.

The next day was much quieter than I thought it would be until we got to lunch. There was a lot of whispering and finger-pointing. Then, I was pulled aside by a very unsuspecting person. The lunch lady. Her name was Mrs. Byers and I will forever owe her a debt of gratitude. She did not hold back any punches and kept calling me son. Now, "Son, what do you think you doing?" I just looked up to her and said nothing. When I say I had to look up to her, that is literal she was a taller lady with that stern look that said don't mess with me. She went on, "Next time you have a problem, slow down it's more people here on your side than those against you. That boy is your brother, not your enemy so go make it right. You do know how to make it right?"I remember saying nope. She then tilted her head and said, "Son you telling me no?" I was like, no, I mean, "I don't know what to do." "how do I know what to say when someone says something bad about my mamma." I don't know what to say to him. She then said something that made me smile and more than anything else, I trusted her. She told me, "Just go apologize. I don't let this happen to my kids at home and it's not going to happen here. That's what some people want you to do: kill each other."

When she said it, she saw that strange look on my face and said, "Yes, I said go to that boy and apologize." Now, I knew she knew or believed in the same thing my Pops did and I could see her as a soldier trying to stop me from getting trapped or shot. A couple of years later, I ended up in a class with her son, but I will talk about that later on. I was just great going forward and a lot of that had to do with seeing her daily.

Things are a little different now at Mrs. Pearls, I guess as time passes and people grow, the things they do change. We weren't playing as much in the street so I found myself wandering to other neighborhoods trying to find some action. One day, I stumbled across a penny that looked really old. I could read the year and it was from 1942. I had seen on TV where real old coins could make you rich and I thought I had found one. I looked left then right, and slid it into my pocket to make sure no one knew I had it. When I got back to Mrs. Pearl, I showed the penny to my sister Bonita. She really didn't make much of it, but I thought telling her would help mend things because we were going to be rich with her and the whole family.

Around the time my mamma picks us up, as it's getting dark. Especially if she worked the cash register at Concord City. Mrs. Pearl is calling for us to come in, and before I get to the driveway, I check for this lottery ticket called a penny. It wasn't there. I began to look around and could not find it. I quickly called Bonita, "You seen my penny?" I asked. She didn't say anything, just tried to walk away. I grabbed her shoulder and asked again, "Did you take my penny?" She pulled away while saying, "Leave me alone." Before I knew it, I was all over her ass. Just swinging, kicking and punching. Mrs. Pearl tried to stop me, but she couldn't then my sis got a lick in and I got even more enraged.

About that time Mrs. Pearl's husband was coming home. I thought he hated all of us anyway, so I could care less about him and I just kept at it till Tyrone held me down. The neighbors had come out and were watching the spectacle. It was a surprise that the police were not called. Needless to say, that was the last day at Mrs. Pearls. I had done it again. My mamma had asked her to watch us as a favor. Her husband didn't want her to have any more kids up in his house. My badass made her breach her word again and now we must go.

Now, I don't know if it was from my previous male posturing or those funny-smelling cigarettes my mamma just smoked; but she took a different approach this time. For the first time in a while she actually held a conversation about what was going on with me. I broke the whole story down to her the same as you read above. I then began to cry. I remember just saying, "I don't know what to do." Like how do I make friends?, how do I be a friend?, "how do I know what to say when someone says something bad." "Who is supposed to teach me." I don't know. This was probably one of the best days of my life.

After that, I became her right hand joining her in the adult choir at church. She said I could join the Rams football team when they started. But most of all, there was this acknowledgment that we were being trapped and shot, there was something at work to divide this black family into as many pieces as possible, starting with creating a fatherless home. This leads to even more division with those who are left as mamma can't do it to the highest level alone. She is forced to leave her nest for hours to make that money and we are left to fend for ourselves. Even if it's against each other.

Mamma must have really taken our conversation to heart and was trying to make as many things right as she had under her control. It was time for the Ram's new season and she was driving me to sign-up. I was so excited I couldn't wait. I think she wanted more than I did, though. She thought it would be a good way to use up energy. We went round and round but could not find the field. After about an hour, we just gave up. Man, I missed it, what the hell, how did we miss it?

The next day I told the gang we tried to make the tryouts but couldn't find it. They said that was the last day to sign up, and I would have to wait another year. I was jacked up. The next week they let me come to one of their practices just to watch. I was excited. When we got there I felt so stupid I finally realized they were not the real Rams. As simple as that seems, this is what happens to young males when there is no one to teach them how things really are. As I watched, I could see why the gang thought I could help them out. I knew I would run all over these guys and they were the best in the area.

I wasn't the only person that was out there watching there was this "North American" girl who looked around my age with red hair. When the guys weren't using the ball we would toss it to each other. I thought she was a tomboy till I threw a hard one, and she couldn't handle it. I mean really bobbled the thing all over the place. Come to find out, she was just watching because she lived next to the field. Actually, the hedges of her yard were right against the field and she had made a playhouse area there. She asked me if I wanted to see, I looked over to the team and they weren't paying me any attention, so I went along. It's funny, once we were in the little playhouse area of the bushes, this girl looked real pretty. I don't know if it was her red hair against the backdrop of the greenery but I thought she was the cutest girl I had ever seen. I can't remember exactly how but we ended up sitting real close. She asked me if I had ever kissed someone. I said no then asked if she had. She said she did once when she was visiting family in Cleveland. Now, I was done and told her I was from Cleveland and had family there, too. Then it happened. We agreed to kiss. Now, me, the expert, closed my eyes and puckered these big lips and headed in. Then she stopped me. I guess she was watching me get prepared. She then asked, "What kind of kiss should we do?" I was like, "What are they?" She replied, "Well in Cleveland I tried to French kiss, it's when our tongues touch." Man, at that point, I was ready to dive into just about anything, you feel me? This was a whole new ballet, and I could tell she was tuned in just like I was. So, we gave it another go. And let me tell you, when those lips met, it was like fireworks, baby! Yup, some tongue action was thrown in for good measure. Now, I swear to you, it felt like it lasted three hours in my mind, but in reality, it had to be about three seconds tops! We locked eyes, looking for that nod of approval, you know? So, we went for it one more time, and this time, I pulled a little move I saw on the tube—touched her chest. She flinched a bit but hey, she rolled with it. Meanwhile, I could hear the team wrapping up practice, and I knew I had to bounce, but I promised, "I'll see you tomorrow."

When I strolled into school the next day, the crew was all buzzing, asking where I'd vanished to during practice. I spilled the story, unaware that some things are better left unsaid. When I mentioned that incident with her chest, someone snickered and asked, "Where else did you touch her?" I was completely lost in the fog of it all, and before I knew it, I was slapped with the moniker "finger fucker." Now, I was a bundle of nerves, worried they would zero in on her for some rough treatment. Funny how I couldn't shake her from my mind since I left, and all I wanted was to defend her honor, to throw a punch at anyone who dared to disrespect her. The rest of the day, I drifted in a haze, lamenting over my own clumsy words—how could I be such a fool? Long story short, that was the last practice I ever attended. Not just out of embarrassment for myself but because I didn't want to bring her any more pain. From then on, those tangled feelings of missing her became my compass for the kind of girl I could really trust with my heart. I promised myself I'd never break that sacred bond again. It felt like a wound that cut deep—what I needed was a father figure to help me navigate through that chaos. It's like life's lessons are making me hurt the very souls I wish to protect. To this day, I still don't know her name, but I'll never forget the vivid image of her radiant red hair.

FAMILY TRUTHS AND ROOTS

My mamma was trying to find ways to make things better for us. Out of her better judgment, my mamma made arrangements for pops to come visit. I know that took a lot out of her, but he came and stayed with us for about three days. We had some good conversations, but three days can't make up for all the lost time. Just seeing how much bigger we had gotten brought tears to his eyes alone. I could see him trying to hold them back. One of the things he made sure I understood, though, was why I may not have the total connection with my big sister and her with me. He was not her biological father. Thus, two firstborns may have been competing for who's first. But as the male, it is my duty, through God, to protect her, which includes from my own hands. I would not see him again for six(6) years. But I really tried to do better for family sake.

Mamma didn't know Pops was going to tell me the truth about Bonita. I was glad he did though. It made me really take a look at not just my life but hers as well. Not only had she been divided from one father figure but a second one as well. That has to be tough. Man, the splitting up of a family is really devastating. When I think about it, only Darren of "Our Gang" has both parents. Going forward, for you folks too young to know, "Our Gang" is old TV show about kids in the hood that we were kinda like. We even had a Darla in Kim Brown and an Alf Alfa in Clarence McGill. Mike, don't get mad, but you were Spanky.

Like most children, the words would sometimes tumble from my lips before I could marshal my thoughts. At home, the pressures were lighter with my sister, but Sundays bore down with a heavy intensity. I recall distinctly a moment after church when both of us endeavored to lay claim to the front seat of the car. It was a seat I was accustomed to, a throne where I'd ensure that both Mother and I donned the finest choir robes, leaping out before the car had fully come to a halt just to race ahead of the elders. But on this day, perhaps the gravity of our return home altered the dynamics. Mamma declared, "Let your big sister take the front." I bristled at the thought of being thrust into a lesser role – I was unaccustomed to being second best, having been rather pampered in those days. And so, as I shuffled to the back, I grumbled under my breath, "She ain't my sister." As I settled into the rear of the car, I felt the weight of Mamma's gaze pierce through me, her voice cutting sharply, "What did you say?" It's easy to feign courage from the backseat. I responded, "Pops said she's my half-sister; she doesn't even know who her daddy is." The expression on my mother's face was a tempest of disbelief and hurt, striking me with such force that a part of me longed to flee from that car and return home. But it was winter's grip that held me firmly in my place, the cold too harsh to brave.

Again, I don't know if it's those funny-smelling little cigarettes my mamma was smoking or church. But that night, while all of us were eating she told Bonita in front of us about her father and how she would try to arrange for her and him to communicate. Come to find out Bonita knew this to be the case way before I opened my fat mouth. But having everything out on the table seems to strengthen us. It was like we were all on the same team now because we all knew what was going on. It was like us coming together, fighting against the things that were trying to divide us. The fighting over food, the fighting over the bathroom, the fighting over the washer, even the TV. all seemed to stop.

The timing for this could not have come at a better time. We began to watch TV together even when mamma was not home. Everything except for "Good Times". We had to compromise on that. I often thought the characters of JJ and Thelma were why we were always fighting, although he was too skinny to be me. But I remember reading in an article in Jet magazine about the dad quitting the show because they kept wanting to portray him as a loser, and he said black men aren't sorry or losers and need to be seen as the strong men they really are. I was done with the show after that. As a compromise, this new show was coming on and Mrs. Cook thought it would be good for us to watch because the annual speech contest was coming up. The name of the show was "Roots." I would bet millions that this show changed the lives of millions. It reaffirmed things brewing in my head and changed my course of life forever. I was so mesmerized I don't think I saw the guys from "our gang" till it was over.

I was Kunta Kinte as a young boy; I had big lips just like him, a nappy afro just like him and really had his pride and love for freedom. I can still hear the music. When the time came to portray Kunta Kinte as a man, they chose Hollywood's number one actor of pride, the father of "Good Times." I am holding back tears now as I picture the scene of them cutting off half his foot to stop him from trying to run away to freedom. This series began to gel our family and again, we were unified in fighting against those who sought to divide us. Those who Opposed Black civil rights, the "D.E.A.D.," were starting to lose ground, and I could feel it, we were finding common ground, no longer satisfied with being on an island.

At school, it was time for the annual "North American" history speech contest and Mrs. Cook was in charge. I remember watching it last year when I first came to the school. The winner went to a kid who just recited the "I Have a Dream" speech. After watching "Roots," I went a different route. I found a big book in the library called "Up from Slavery" by Booker T. Washington. He did not have any speeches that I could recite but the book was full of ideas about blacks as a people that I thought most had not heard about. It was very similar to that of "Roots". I was especially intrigued by his thoughts about "White Boys" and how he wanted to be like them because of their ancestry. But when he realized the "White Boy" had to live up to their families' expectations, he realized this was not what was designed for him as the status of his family's historical expectations. It actually would be counterproductive to him and his people's entire existence. This led me to a clearer understanding that I am still metamorphosing, as that is what a "North American" is, made up of all mankind on this land called North America.

When time came to sign up for the contest, I could tell by the look on Mrs. Cook's face that I was not on her radar as a potential winner. She actually didn't pay me any attention; just took my slip while talking to some of the others. Now, you know I thrive on that Ahhh Ha moment, so I did research and learned my speech word for word with a plan to walk away from the podium while saying my speech. I blew em away. I had to perform multiple times for multiple groups before I came home with the trophy. This was a first for me and it was like I was groomed to do just that: speak about the discourse of others for the benefit of others.

After my speech, something shifted in the room—a

heaviness lifted, and then my mother let slip a secret she had tucked away, a whisper from her past. The man we all knew as granddaddy J.D. was not her father at all; instead, there was a photograph revealed, a man named Robinson. His image lingered there, an echo of history. Like my sister, my mother had navigated life with a certain detachment, the absence of both parents creating a chasm we barely understood. Realization dawned like the soft light of dawn breaking through sheer curtains—I had to shatter this cycle, this inheritance of pain. The dysfunction that ran through our family felt palpable, almost like a character in a film casting long shadows over our lives.

In preparing for my speech, I thought about Booker T. and the absence of family that left him grappling with the simplest rituals—table manners, personal hygiene, the intimacy of routine. Now, I find myself echoing his struggles; my mouth bears witness to years of neglect—rotten teeth like characters in a silent film, shoes worn until they barely hold their shape. It's a cycle I cannot perpetuate; the desire to redefine my narrative swells within me, a quiet rebellion against the ghosts of our past.

The first step in making change is to have a clear understanding of your adversary. When I chose to do my speech on Booker T. vs. Martin Luther King's "I Have a Dream" speech. I leaned on conversations I overheard at my uncle Buddy's barbershop. I often heard the guys talking about how there were just as many, if more, people who were offended and threatened by his speech than those who actually liked it. Some of them were even saying had he not threatened Congress and the Senate in the speech he might be alive today.

THE MUHAMMAD ALI CONFIDENCE

Float like a butterfly Sting like a bee it's time for desegregation Fergie. I was on a roll. I had a lot of positive things happening in my life. I loved my trophy and mounted it on TV. I didn't know what being conceited meant but this is what my sister was starting to call me. I was starting to grow and was doing push ups and getting stronger. I would sing this song while looking at myself in the mirror, "Float like a butterfly sting like a bee. I am the greatest because my name is Fergie." It was sweet. Confidence was not something I was lacking at that time.

The championship matches for wrestling were in the morning before school. I was singing my song all morning trying to get hype as I was in the championship match. I had a special drink I would make in my special jug. On this morning when I went to the refrigerator to get my jug it was empty. It was on the table so I grabbed it and started to make my Kool-Aid and Tang mix all over again. When I turned my back to get sugar my sister had grabbed it and was pouring out my "tang". Then the shit started, "You don't own it', we can all use it". I just snatched it from her, "You know that's been my jug. I even drink straight from the top, lips all over it." She then tried to snatch it from me. Girl too slow as I moved quickly away. I had said I wouldn't fight her anymore. Then out of the side of my eye, I saw a knife coming right at me. She was swinging it like a crazy man. And then it happened, right? Instead of going for a swing, she decides to make this wild, stabbing motion at my arm. Too slow, though. This time, she wasn't quick enough for me. She missed my arm, but got my wrist! Blood started gushing out like I just walked into a damn horror movie. I looked down and felt like I was in a medical drama, thinking, "Am I about to see my bone, for real?" But here's the kicker—I found myself worried about two things, man. First, I didn't want her to get in hot water over this. I mean, it was serious! And second? I was stressing about that championship match like it was the Super Bowl of my life.

I remember seeing something on TV where a guy glued his cut close. I quickly ran cold water on it till I could see the white meat. Then I pinched it close. I was too scared to put a needle through it because it was about two inches long and that would take too long and just be too many holes I would have to make on my wrist. So, I got some of that Christmas tape and put it across the cut, then added glue all over my wrist and the tape. I put some tissue on to soak up any extra blood then wrapped it with an ace bandage and a wristband.

I was good and hustled to the school. I made it to the match just in time and pinned my opponent in less than a minute. "Float like a butterfly sting like a bee thank God for stopping my cut from really bleeding. "I never told on her, I guess that talk I had with pops gave me a real change of heart. Just too bad I had to get the scare of my life to remind me of how much I did love me, sis. But man have we fallen into the tramp. We been shot by the "D.E.A.D". This is exactly what the results of a divided family would bring. Family members killing each other so they wouldn't have to. Under the grace of

God through the prayers of others I survived again, but how many more lives would I have? It's time for me to really find focus because I'm about to be placed in the trenches of the Desegregation movement. I am going to be used with the white kids.

The courts had ordered that the "North American" kids of Townview would now merge with the white kids of Trotwood. The only way to get us there would be by bus. This would be my first ever school bus ride. The gang was going to Junior High School. Man, what a building it was all glass. This is how white folks go to class. The first day everyone was really feeling each other out and this included the teachers. Today I am an educator so I know what we should not do to kids. There were some obvious great things going on there but they were mixed in with a lot of stereotypes.

The principal was a familiar face, Mr. Cook, the husband of my elementary teacher. This made me feel like I had an upper hand since I just made his wife seem like a genius by winning the speech contest and she was also a member of my church. Then the obvious happened, the "D.E.A.D" would put their footprint on us. I saw it but I didn't know if the others thought of it the way I did. We were broken up into four sections joining both the 7th and 8th graders together. The first class was Alpha, the second class was Beta, the third class was Theta/Kappa and the fourth class was Delta. When I saw this I immediately said I guess they didn't need anything after that because those kids would be zeroes and called Phi, or some Greek word past the letter "F". For some reason, I was taught about the Greek alphabet when I was in East Cleveland. I had two table mates from different communities, both 8th graders. Maurice Douglas and the son of my elementary school lady of authority Keith Byers. Both are pictured below.

CURSE OF THE BELLY DANCER SEX & RACISM

My family, though once scattered like leaves upon the wind, found itself woven together in a strange fondness during that fateful winter. Then came a storm—a tempest of snow and ice, as fierce as any tale spun by the fireside. The record-setting blizzard of 1978, while fearsome to some, felt like a grand adventure to me, for it meant missing school, a rare gift in our lives. The icy world outside became a frosty kingdom, too treacherous for the likes of us to be in, but the pause from our daily duties was a welcome reprieve. Our kind neighbor, with her heart full and her belly round, often called upon me for aid, requesting that I wield my trusty shovel to clear her driveway, for she was unable to brave the depths of winter with her belly swelled to an impressive size with a human inside. She would dance for me, and in those moments, we shared a connection—a bond woven through abdominal movement and delight. She was a true belly dancer, clad in shimmering chains that jingled about her waist and adorned with sparkling gems nesting in her navel. Quite the sight, indeed! To my surprise, she treasured my thoughts on her graceful sways, especially regarding that marvelous belly of hers.

When the time came for her to welcome her little one into the world. There was not a soul present except for my dear Mother. In the midst of directing the ambulance, however, she slipped upon a treacherous patch of ice, and lo! Her knee met with a most unfortunate fate. When the paramedics finally arrived, they were led to believe they might have to guide a new life into the light, yet found themselves hurrying both her and my dear mother to the hospital instead. Mother's injury proved grave indeed, and she lingered in the hospital for what felt like a long stretch, a whole week by my count. Yet, in that time, we—those spirited Ferguson children—managed to hold down the fort, standing watch and caring for one another like brave hobbits in a great adventure, steadfast in our task

I found myself in quite a precarious situation, hovering at the edge of youthful hormonal change. Ah, the whims of young maidens—I had no wise mentor by my side to guide me through this maze of emotions. My own feelings were like a wild storm, tempestuous and unrelenting. Mornings left me startled at the strength of my own heart's yearnings, and with naught but a simple house phone, I clung to it as if it were the One Ring, ever longing for connection. Alas, I was utterly lost! My heart, unsteady in its bearings, was ill-prepared for the throngs of affection that besieged me. When a maid would gaze upon me and inquire if I wished to be her suitor, I foolishly acquiesced, utterly unaware of the true weight of such a commitment. Suddenly, I was entangled with Charlotte, Janis, Tonya, Michelle, and Sonja—each beckoning to me, and thus I opened my heart to a multitude of feelings. Yet, with every flutter, I found myself wrestling with emotions that spiraled beyond my grasp, and inevitably heart began to crack under the strain of my inexperience. The gravest peril lay in the thought of fatherhood, a daunting path devoid of guiding stars. I stood on the brink, ill-prepared for the responsibility that loomed ever closer.

In those days, when the shadow of unthinking decisions loomed heavy like a dark cloud, I found myself curious, well-suited to bring ruin upon any girl in my path. The D.E.A.Ds, sinister as a wraith, had me firmly in their sights, ready to strike. Yet, amid this impending doom, a little redhead emerged as a beacon—a spark of hope in a realm fraught with peril. Each time I neared the brink, thoughts of her would flood my mind, reminding me of the pain I had wrought upon her heart. It was enough to jolt me back to reality. After my spirit had whispered "no" to temptation for the third time, clarity washed over me: she was no mere mishap, but rather a guiding light placed on my path—not solely to save my own soul, but to shield others from the harm I might have inflicted.

The next season of football brought forth the stirrings of tension that lay beneath the surface, much like the shadows that dance upon the hills of Middle-earth. At long last, our community was seen with the hopeful glint of a championship team—like the light of a star piercing through the darkness. Playing time became as precious as a rare gem. My heart sang for the game itself, blissfully unaware of the difference between practice and the grand quest of a match. As long as there was a ball I was content. Every so often, one stumbles upon a moment of clarity, an "ah-ha!" realization that brightens the dullest of practices. I had mine, though it came at the expense of poor Ben Gordon, whose struggle would be a tale of its own.

After the practice, we were walking back to the locker room. I was naive and did not know this cat was really embarrassed as his father watched the practice. Our gang overheard his father talk about his dissatisfaction and they had dealt with him in the past. They were telling me, "Ferg, don't turn your back on him. Whatever you do, don't turn your back on him." I paid it no attention. Sure, enough with pads and everything, this cat hits me square in the spine, my head does a whiplash backward then I hit the ground. Now, we are still a team so no one is going to get in to help the other guy so I am in it all by myself. He made a huge mistake and let me take my helmet off before he hit me. I was able to get to my knees while he was hitting me from behind and I had just enough room to wack this fool with my helmet. Then I felt a rage kick in and I started going to town on this fool. Shit, I had never lost a fight and wasn't about to lose one now. Once I got the upper hand, they broke it up. Then the gang broke it down to me that they had been dealing with this kind of shit from him and a couple of others since pee-wee ball. I let them know that where I am from, we don't take shit like that from white people. This was the first time an acknowledgment that I was from somewhere different was on the table and I took great pride in being from East Cleveland, Ohio. The word the next day was that his father kicked his ass for losing to a nigger.

A couple of months later, I had a run-in with both he and his dad but this time I was really alone. The rest of the gang was playing basketball while I decided to go out for the wrestling team. Wouldn't you know it? Me and him were in the same weight class and only one person could represent the school. In the wrestle off I beat his ass easily and in front of his racist as daddy. The next day at the match, I pinned my opponent in under 15 seconds. I think the kid was afraid just because I was "North American," and prior to desegregation, "North American" and "American" didn't wrestle each other in that area.

After the match, the "American" coach had to drive me home. I really felt uncomfortable with that but it was my only way home. This happened two more times after practice and the third time, I lied and said I had a ride, then walked home. I didn't realize it then but after checking our modern-day

Mapquest it says it's about 12 miles from the school at 3594 North Snyder Road, Trotwood to 5225 Rucks Rd. I lied about having a ride home again the next day but this time, I decided to cut through the old corn field that was behind my home. The ground was so wet my jeepers were soaked. The wind was blowing so hard that the snot from my nose was freezing. There was like a little mirage of trees in the middle of the field and I had to stop. There are three times in my life when I really believe I died and this was the first. Till today the last thing I remember is lying down next to one of the trees to block the wind and then falling asleep. I can't remember how I got home. Nonetheless that was my sign, so I quit the wrestling team, which also took the stress off from Ben and his father.

The very next day, the coach approached Mr. Cook, declaring with a rather firm resolve, "I quit." It was as if he spoke those words with the intention of having Mr. Cook sway me back into the fold, which indeed was his pursuit. After Mr. Cook had a word with me, and I stood my ground about not wrestling, he took it upon himself to administer a paddling. Perhaps I ought to have mentioned my discomfort at the thought of riding home with the coach or traipsing those many miles alone. I held out hope that he would grasp the gravity of my feelings without my needing to explain them. Alas, that was not the case, and the air grew thick with tension. At that moment, I felt like I was standing on the brink of something tragic — the specter of "D.E.A.D" loomed large. It was, without a doubt, a betrayal of the deepest sort; it was merely him and me in that room, and whatever message he sought to convey would find its mark solely upon me. My mind was aflame with images from the television series Roots, where the injustices and hatred spewed forth by Ben Gordon flashed vividly in my thoughts—my heart held captive by the fact that the hand raised against me was that of a "North American" man, simply because I had not complied with the wishes of the "American" man. I cast a long and wistful gaze at the scissors resting on his desk. Good grief! My own father had never laid a hand on me, despite my reckless folly of trying to stab a child. At that moment, all respect and trust in him crumbled; the proud spirit of Ferguson coursed through me, ignited by "D.E.A.D." I felt an undeniable rift growing between my kin in C-town and the elder ones in Dayton. Yet still, us young ones were like a fellowship unto ourselves, gathering to share our thoughts on safe sex, fraternity, and unity. As we navigated a world our parents had scarcely known because of Desegregation, we found strength in the expanding library of knowledge we were weaving together. It felt magical, a treasure yet undiscovered

It was time to move on to High School. The July the summer of 1979. The King brothers Derrick and Kevin moved into the neighborhood and quickly fit right in as they loved to play football and had a basketball hoop in the backyard. Month 1 of 24 straight months in school begins. People are really taking notice of what was athletically occurring at Trotwood due to busing. The words Dynasty are starting to be used, and egos getting high. The West Carrollton community has been the only blemish on the record and I missed that game both in the 7th and 8th grades. I actually had never had the feeling that comes with a loss. This really set a value for the rest of my life.

Once the season started, things really started to change. I was adopted as the little brother by the upperclassmen in the neighborhood. It got to the point where I was not even riding the bus but was given rides. Charles Byrd was his name, he was the star running back on varsity. He had this cool orange and white two-door Pinto. Then there was the other Fergie. He was a starter on the basketball team. He was lanky, tall, with long arms and had a deadly turn-around jump shot. His teammate on varsity was the Hawk, Trannel Hawkins, man could this guy jump? The five of us were always hitching a ride with the Byrd man. It made me feel real cool but more importantly, I had to be mature. We were in this together as they would talk about what they were doing on the field and on the court.

There was a bit of chatter among the lads about the fair games I had been playing. At long last, I was given a chance to tread the fields, truly, in the backfield, and even more thrilling, I would face the rival Northmont in a rare night match. They expressed their pride in my efforts, and I felt a great weight upon my shoulders—the wish to not let them down. That was the day my understanding of the game deepened, like finding a hidden path in the woods. The coach's pre-game words echoed in my heart, words that I would carry with me through many seasons. He had a way of looking straight into our eyes, and I made sure to meet his gaze with my own. He began to challenge us, saying, "All of you looking into my eyes right now are not ready, not ready to face the battle that awaits." I felt a jolt at his doubt. He continued, "If you aren't so furious that it brings a tear to your eye, you are mistaken. Tears should fall from your face, not out of sorrow, but from a fire within, the flame of anger against those who mean to hurt you, to hurt your kin." He insisted, "If you are not mad enough to weep with fury, I can guarantee that they shall triumph, laughing as they impose their will upon you, leaving you to shed tears of defeat." And oh, how my heart surged with rage, my vision blurred from the intensity of it. He spotted me, holding back the waves of emotion, and his finger pointed my way as he declared, "He's ready." That day, amidst the roars of the crowd and the clashing of wills, I played the game of my life. At long last, I discovered the edge that had been waiting, just beyond the Shire horizon.

The school was loaded with kids but kids just kept moving

in. Then it happened, for the first time in my life, someone cleaned my clock. He hit me so hard my nose started bleeding. It was like something out of the "Rocky" movies. I thought I had played against the best when we would scrimmage the JV team, and they were loaded with players. My Delta classmates Maurice Douglas and Keith Byers (pictured above) were both on that squad. Mo was the running back and Keith was the tight end. I had to tackle them both and man, did that hurt. But what happened to me on this day was different. A new kid had just transferred in and was out to show he could ball. What better way than to knock out the leading rusher from the last game? His name was Dwight Sistrunk, his uncle was a real nasty lineman for the NFL Oakland Raiders, so they say. This was really the last piece of a dynasty. We all knew that when everyone finally got on the same team, no one in the nation, let alone the state, would be able to beat us. However, a mother's love for her children would come to split up what should have been a dynasty. I moved back to Cleveland over Christmas break. Keith transferred to Dayton Roth of Dayton public schools and later went on to have successful careers in the NFL (pictured above). Amazingly 14 of us went on to become coaches, and produced professional athletes, but that's another story.

Members of C.O.R.K. (Citizens Opposed to Rearranging Kids) protest along the Detroit-Superior Bridge prior to the start of the school year in 1979.

FACE TO FACE WITH THE "D.E.A.D."

There exists no bond quite like that of a mother's love, fiercely protective, instinctively aware, sensing the tremors of danger that cause the earth beneath her cubs to shift. In the quiet of what appeared to be normalcy, the "D.E.A.D"'s worked tirelessly, their aims obscured by the daily minutiae. Through it all, I came to understand that a mother's most potent weapon was prayer—an invocation, a plea to the universe. For my mother and dear Mrs. Byers, those prayers found their footing in the world, manifesting in blessings untold. After the knee injury, my mother felt a vulnerability that made her yearn for solace of her own — a pull toward familiarity and kinship. So, she sought a civil service position in Cuyahoga County, the beating heart that served the city of Cleveland, Ohio. The time had come for us to return home. Yet, with this homecoming lurked the weight of unspoken burdens. The same exodus from Trotwwod was true for Keith, a robust boy with hands as deft as his speed and by standout Derrick Jones, both set to grace Dayton Roth. For now, my journey led me to Cleveland, Ohio, a new chapter woven into the tapestry of stories yet to unfold.

The "D.E.A.D"s were determined to keep "North Americans" and "Americans" in their own Cleveland neighborhoods despite the integration success stories in other cities like Dayton and Columbus. Clevelanders were determined to not let folks cross the bridge. Some were so adamant that they formed their own ghost title in an effort to lure support. It was called C.O.R.K. (citizens opposed to rearranging kids) (pictured above). The east and west sides of Cleveland are divided by the Cuyahoga River. The "North Americans" lived on the Eastside and the "Americans" on the Westside. Their protest would come to a head at the bridge most notably called the Detroit/Superior bridge.

During this time of protest, the teachers had decided to strike. The strange and most dangerous part was you could not visually identify who was opposing the unification because the protesters were teachers, cops, politicians, business owners, bus drivers, firemen, priests, doctors, lawyers and the list goes on.

While I was in classes and on the playing field at Trotwood Madison High School, 101,000 kids in Cleveland were all just sitting at home while all of this got sorted out. This fight would go on strongly for another six years. Before it all came to a head, we witnessed heart-wrenching tragedies—suicides that left scars, riots echoing the struggles of our past, and the rise of violent gangs that sought to fill a void. These times were reminiscent of the turbulent 60s, yet the violence unfolded in hushed tones, behind closed doors. We were without the immediacy of social media or the omnipresence of cellphone cameras, which meant that much of the pain and unrest went unnoticed by the wider public. Just like the stock market, our social fabric experienced its own rollercoaster of highs and lows. When teachers made the courageous decision to return to work, I found myself standing in the thick of it all —facing questions that have lingered for over four decades:

Why me? Why was I positioned at this intersection of history and upheaval?

It's Christmas break 1979 but instead of wrapping gifts we were wrapping up and packing up our house. It was time to go. This move was odd for me as it's the first time I didn't do anything to make us have to move so I thought. So I held a lot of resentment for breaking up my future path to the NFL. Our society has some jacked-up ways. One of those was choosing what to value, and to our detriment, we place a lot of value on being a star. That was one of the baits that the "D.E.A.D." threw at our community in the 60s. Now, I was old enough to want to eat this bait. I was full of so much stimulation for the Trotwood football hype, I just knew I was going to the NFL. I was now watching the NFL on TV not because of what they were doing but because of what I was going to do to them when I got there.

I felt as if I was moving backward. Let me take you back five months. August 1, 1979. It is the first day of high school football. I have arrived. My classes are good; I'm acing them, A's and B's. On the field, I am alive, and at home, there are no fights, no trouble. Fast forward five months. I find myself among the younger ones, the seventh and eighth graders. No football team, no bus rides, no girls, just the stale air of a mundane school day. January 1980. Lincoln Junior High in Cleveland, Ohio. We moved back just in time; the teacher's strike ended, but it felt like a step back.

Having been a part of the Dayton desegregation movement with positive results she tried to keep us integrated by moving to the west side of the river also known as the Tremont side. What ma to grasp in that moment was that this was not the "North American" community of the familiar faces I had come to know in Trotwood; no, this was a community marked by poverty, primarily Latino, a reality I had never truly encountered before. I found myself asking, where in the world have I been? Just when you believe you have a grasp on the circumstances around you, life unveils an entirely new realm of existence. Is this the norm? This question echoed in my mind, a relentless inquiry that persisted for an entire month. I began to sense a troubling notion—that this experience was crafted uniquely for me, and it was incumbent upon me to seek out the purpose behind it all.

Welcome To Our New Principal Mr. Sampson

A year is a space in time, it has no significance without events and activities. A yearbook is such a record of the activities and events that have enriched the lives of those involved. This yearbook should etch into our memories many precious moments and many delightful experiences we have all shared at Lincoln-West High School. I consider it an honor and a privilege to be a part of these activities and the memories we share together. The school is important, but the individuals are our most treasured possessions. I trust that as the future unfurls we will have used our experiences here to provide us with the necessary skills required to become productive and useful citizens of our great country. Each of you have played a part in making our school and community a place loved, respected, and cherished by those this book is dedicated to honor.

Joseph Sampson, Principal

BOOKER T. AND ME

My new school was within walking distance from the new crib. But what a shocker. Walking to school was like walking a gauntlet of people shooting at you or so that's how it felt. On both sides of the street, there were nothing but "American" people or Latinos, not a single "North American" person. This was a first for me and every eye that looked at my cocoa brown skin made me get in the defensive mode. It was like I was the first person of color they had seen walking their streets.

My hope was that I would have at least one teacher that I could relate to like in the past. Well, no luck on that. I was by myself. On the second day, some strange looking man came to my class and had me come to his office. I had never seen anyone that looked like him before. His hair was not like that of a "North American" or "American" person, behind his glasses his eyes had a slight slant like Asians but that was not it. It was utterly fascinating, really—he had my complete focus, and you could say I was all ears. Right there in front of him was a folder that turned out to contain my records from Trotwood. I had him in a bit of a bind, you see, because I had already nailed down half a school year's worth of work, boasting all As and Bs. Quite a remarkable feat, while the rest of the school hadn't seen much success—what can I say, I was eager to play fair! With a smile, he called me "son," much like Mrs. Byers had done, and then introduced himself: "I'm Joseph Sampson, the principal here." I must have worn a look on my face that said, "What's the scoop?" because he quickly reassured me, "You're not in trouble; I'm just scouting for some leaders, and I like what I see in your grades." He leaned forward, curiosity twinkling in his eyes. "Where are you from —not your school, I've got that covered." So, I unraveled my story for him, the journey from East Cleveland to Dayton, Trotwood, and now back to Cleveland. He nodded, a knowing smile tugging at the corners of his mouth. "You're like me, with roots planted in many places." "I'm an Indian; some prefer 'Native American,' but you can relax. I'm on your side." There was a warmth in his tone as if he truly understood the weight of it all. "I need you to keep up that fantastic work ethic you had at your last school and reach out to as many of the other kids as you can this week. Can you do that for me?" I didn't hesitate, a simple "sure" escaping my lips. He beamed, handing me a pass back to class. At that moment, I felt a little rush of pride, a little boost to my ego; I was no longer just chasing grades for myself but for him as well. It was as if I had tapped into something new—a shared ambition.

On the way home it dawned on me. When I was getting ready for my speech on Booker T. Washington, I learned that he lived with a group of Native American Indian men as a "house father," where he gave the inspiration of education especially on the industrial side. Had this now come full circle and the Indian was helping the black man.

The morning sun spilled through the school windows, and the teachers—oh, they were lookin' at me in a way that felt like I'd been branded. Like a whisper in the hall had set the wheels turnin'. Then it struck me, fate strummin' its guitar. I found myself in his office, the air thick with unspoken words. You could sense his frustration, but all I could do was hope it wasn't aimed at me. He asked if I'd found a friend, and sure enough, I had—easy as singin' a verse. He dropped a bomb—Lincoln was my home and new kids from places far away were supposed to join the scene. I thought, "Hey, that's cool." But then came the heavy hand on my shoulder, "Son, I need you to help everyone find common ground." Little did he know, he was askin' me to dance on the edge, life's gamble at play. From that moment on, everything changed, like a song turned upside down. The teachers were back to their routines, but the kids, they hadn't all found their paths in this new world born from a court's decree. Fear lingered in the air, thick enough to choke the spirit outta Cleveland, Mr. Sampson among them, and there I was, a beacon, a bridge he dreamed I could be. Just like that, I aged overnight—took on a weight that felt heavier than a world on my shoulders.

The brother and the sisters came by the bus load. It was rather exciting. They all came from different neighborhoods and didn't all know each other as well. This made it easy for me to just kick it with everyone. Then I got some help from an unlikely source; A gang actually. All of us were able to relate to this gang, as for the first time someone was saying something that was meant for all of us. I still remember it today and I actually tell it to my own kids as well as students. It went like this:

I said a hip-hop
Hippie to the hippie
The hip, hip a hop and you don't stop a rock
to the bang bang boogie, boobie to the boogie
To the rhythm of the boogie, the beat

Now, what you hear is not a test. I'm rappin' to
    the beat
And me, the groove, and my friends are gonna try to
    move your feet
See, I am Wonder Mike, and I'd like to say hello
To the black, to the white, the red and the brown
The purple and yellow, but first, I gotta
Bang bang, the boogie to the boogie
Say up, jump the boogie, to the bang bang boogie
Let's rock, you don't stop
Rock the rhythm that'll make your body rock
Well so far you've heard my voice, but I brought two
    friends.

That's right, the Sugar Hill Gang brought the words "black, to the white, the red and the brown, the purple and yellow;" to the table and that covered all of us. It was mandatory that mamma had to buy us that album. It was like the whole city was now repeating the words. When Mr. Sampson saw that this song/music/rap was unifying the kids which ultimately flowed to the community and we had monthly dances just to keep the momentum moving.

Now, it would seem as if the "D.E.A.D"s were losing momentum but that was not the case. You add popularity with a party and a new face and you come up with Girls Girls Girls. Here we go again. Minerva Pachekels and Lucy Ivory. One Hispanic and one "North American". I had to once again be saved by that redhead. This recipe was perfect for me to be a father at that time. I had a girl who would do anything and I mean anything just to be my girl and giving me the pootinanny was one. Pootinanny is my word pussy. Man, it was close. But I knew I wasn't about to grow old and grey with this girl and the guys were already asking if I hit it. I thought about what I had done to the redhead and for the first time, I broke things off with a girl. It wasn't long before I had another one. maybe an hour. Hey, I was young.

This girl Lucy was cool, from the other side of town, a vibe I ain't never felt before. I was intrigued, man, it had me hooked. I'd hop on the bus with her, rollin' through streets I ain't familiar with, then footin' it for two hours back home. Some things shift, but the essence stays the same, you know? I was like Cain on "Kung Fu," just wanderin' and searchin' for something. And her mom, Flo, she was a whole vibe, feeding me like I was family. I was livin' the dream, but every good saga hits a pause. Easter break hit, and I was eager to vibe with Lucy and her crew. Then I got hit with the news—they planned a trip to Cincinnati, and I was just a ghost in their plans. Walking up to their crib, they looked at me like I was in the know: "Larry, you ride in the back." No questions asked, just assumptions flying, like I was part of the crew already. Just like that, I'm off to Cincinnati, while the world outside doesn't even know if I exist. Before the days of cell phones and the internet, life was raw, man. The whole scene with folks in the hood, it was a tight-knit bond born out of survival, especially since the system dismantled the family vibes back in the day. They didn't even think to ask if I had my people's blessing to roll out. Matter of fact, they never even inquired if I had parents; it was easier for them to just let it be, a silent understanding on this wild ride.

Now, we have only been back in Cleveland for about three months and I done gone missing with all this hatred going around. It's Easter and mamma is taking the family to church but has no idea where I am at and that was the last thing on my mind. I was with a real family. This girl had a brother, mother and a father; and they all liked me. Luckily, the family we went to visit thought the whole thing looked suspicious. They then insisted that I call a parent from their phone. That was right on time, as when mamma pick it up the phone she was on the verge of calling the police. Her child was missing for two days. The phone call also saved me from that beatdown. I think then was when my mamma realized that I really desired to be around folks like me. Although I was cool with the folks in the neighborhood, I was still this kid who studied Booker T. Washington for the purpose of giving words about my people to my people.

Afterward, it became astonishingly apparent that she had been beseeching the heavens on my behalf, for not long after my solemn introspection, I found myself at a gathering not far from Lucy's quaint abode. Amidst the revelry, the boy who accompanied me approached with an almost conspiratorial air, proffering a diminutive shard of aluminum foil. "Here, man, take a hit of this—it's coke," he declared, his tone laced with naïve bravado. Instantly, my mind drifted back to the grim spectacle of "The FBI" on screen, juxtaposed against the haunting finale of "Lady Sings the Blues." In my youthful folly, one conjured images of cold iron bars while the other echoed tales of lives meticulously squandered amid the debris of unfulfilled dreams. "No, man," I retorted, an instinctual dread clawing at my insides. Driven by a morbid curiosity, I probed, "Why would you poison yourself with that stuff?" He replied with eager enthusiasm that it would elevate his performance, for he yearned to entwine his voice with the pulsating heartbeat of music that night. There I stood, enveloped in a basement that could very well serve as a graveyard of potential—each face a harbinger of the endless cycle that would ensnare them in the clutches of the "D.E.A.D." My heart clenched at the vivid tableau of despair, a tableau I would not soon forget. I comprehended then, with a pang of melancholy, that the very fabric of our community was woven with the threads of entrapment, and at the tender age of fourteen, no one dared to intervene. That melancholy revelation marked the last of my ventures into that forsaken part of town.

I did see Lucy again, some twenty (20) years at a house party the night, me and my wife decided to make my third child Taylorblair. She was with her husband who I found a bit strange, so strange God wouldn't let me shake his hand. A couple years later I performed some pre-sentence investigation work on him for a judge. The fool was video-taping Lucy's daughter and friends while they were showering; a straight-up pervert. He did get some jail time and eventually committed suicide. God is good.

THE BIG "AAAAAHS…"

By the end of June, I was tired though. I was really starting to lose that positive energy. The walkabouts had stopped, I have been dealing with some sort of school activity since August and school was extended till the end of July to make up for the time school was closed due to the strike. Mr. Sampson could see I was getting tired. In an effort to keep me going I was put with the honors group of kids along with a change of schedule that had me in industrial arts classes. I was then placed on the National Junior Honor Society and asked to help tutor and help kids who were struggling. Now, this is the kid who was placed in Delta and the academically slow group while in Dayton. But here in Cleveland, I am an academic star. It did help my ego for about a month then it happened again. I liked the freedom to move around the school because of the tutoring and stuff.

It was the summertime and the PE classes were starting to go outside. One day, I noticed they had a ball, a football. I watched from afar and noticed they were playing real soft, like when I was in the 5th grade, I wanted no part of that. I actually needed some competition. While I was watching them one of the industrial arts teachers was watching me. Mr. Sovchik was his name. He asked me, "Why don't you go over there and play." I got in my Ali arrogant tone and said, "Play what that" "They not doing anything." Now, he obviously thought I was joking and took offense to the comment. He had one of the kids throw him the ball. Then he played like he couldn't throw it back and handed it to me. I threw a dart, the ball was only about 5 feet off the ground and traveled about 40 yards.

Mr. Sovchik would do this thing with his lips when he was puzzled. He then goes, "You are a good quarterback." I then broke it down to him, I aback both linebacker and running back and they couldn't all handle me if they were on one team" One of the kids overheard me and said, "Come on out here then"

Now, I hadn't done anything since the season ended and hadn't even talked to anyone about Trotwood but knew they couldn't stop me or get by me. So, it was one(1) against 7 and I got the ball first. Mistake number one, they throw the ball to me straight down the middle. I picked out their two guys in the middle and ran straight at them. Now, this is not the head injury concussion era and at Trotwood, we had no problem lowering that head. I think the first kid I got to thought I was going to slow down and make a move because he slowed down. Big mistake, I dropped my head dead center of his chest. I could hear the air leave his body. It felt so good. One other person tried grabbing my arm and all he could do was scratch me. Yea, I was bleeding from the scratch but I scored. After a few minutes, they helped the first kid get into the gym. Shit, I didn't care.

The kid who jumped in to help? Yeah, he bailed, and suddenly it was me against a mob of five. I could see it in their eyes—fear mixed with boredom, like they were just stalling for time, not really into the game. I whipped the ball to the guy closest to me on my left, and then I was off, jogging right like some kind of action hero. This dude figured he could score quick, booking it down what we called the sideline—like it was some sacred space, but really just a patch of dirt alongside the fence separating us from Clark Avenue. Now, here's the kicker: over the years, I somehow developed this freakish ability to kick into high gear when I was chasing someone with the ball. And damn, I hit this kid so hard we became one like white on rice—his head, his shoulders, his whole deal, just flying toward that fence. Suddenly, the ball's loose, I'm diving for it, and the crowd erupts with a collective AAAhh. Oh, that sound? It's music to my ears. But then, out of nowhere, I catch a brand new sound—like the world's weirdest cross between an OOH and a full-on scream. Confused, I look up, and they're all pointing at me. That's when I saw it—a wine bottle sent flying over the fence, exploded upon impact. I crash to the ground, and that sharp glass slices into my right thigh, blood everywhere. Honestly? I didn't even feel it. But the panic on everyone else's faces? Priceless. They're all hustling me toward the nurse's office, but in my mind, I'm still fixated on one thing: did I win?

The school nurse put some gauze and tape on it and because it was the end of the day, told me to have my mom take me to the hospital to get stitches. They had no idea, I had my own remedy of glue and tape. It only left a little scar. Mamma never knew what happened. The next day I was both a football star and tough man. Then I came to find out Mr. Sovchik was the Head Football Coach at the high school it was the middle of the summer and she was getting ready for the first desegregated team in school history. He quickly gave me all of the information I needed for the team tryouts the following week.

A NEW OUR GANG...

The high schools were faced with so many threats of violence and withdrawal of students that their full implementation of the desegregation order would not take place until the start of the next school year. That time was now upon us. Mr. Sampson had presented our successful integration at Lincoln Jr. to the school with enough flair that Mr. Sampson and Mr. Sovchik were assigned to Lincoln-West High School with me.

Because I was playing football the process for me was very much like the last. Practice began on August 1st only a week after the end of school. I was now on my 13th consecutive month of school. Many of the players that were to be bus to Lincoln-West were trying their best to stay with their neighborhood team. Many had been working out with them in hopes that the whole thing was just a dream and one day they would wake up and still be Tarblooders or Hornets. On the first day of practice, there were some black players though. Some had been given the opportunity to voluntarily go to schools on the other side of town. This had been a failed attempt to curve the court order by saying nothing was stopping "North Americans" from going to school with "Americans" other than the decision by "North Americans" themselves. The courts did not buy this and nonetheless, those kids got to stay. One in particular caught my attention. He was senior and they treated him like royalty. The star running Bubba Ken Stanback.

Imagine, if you will, a grand tableau where acres of green grass and cornfields would seem like a distant memory. Enter Lincoln-West High School, a concrete monolith set against a backdrop of homes as unyielding as they are uninspired. No lush lawns here—just a sprawling expanse of cement that starkly contrasted the pastoral charm I once knew. The nearest hint of nature lay only down by the sand mines, where a gargantuan smokestack puffed and wheezed its noxious breath, day in and day out. Now, to make our way to the fields, we had to muster ourselves into a double file—yes, safety first, I suppose. Helmets firmly strapped on, we were instructed not to remove them until we reached our destination. And so commenced our two-mile jog, a veritable gauntlet through unfamiliar streets inhabited by those who seemed less than thrilled by our very presence—like unwelcome guests at a party awkwardly clutching their drinks. Ah, but the pièce de résistance came when we crossed the bridge over the I-71 highway—what a sight! We might as well have been circus performers enhancing the local entertainment. All the while, the neighborhood spectators would watch us, eyes wide and curious, as if we were some peculiar creatures at the zoo, the kind nobody paid to see. The irony wasn't lost on me; after practice, the entire ordeal would repeat, echoing like a refrain from a tragic play. There were moments I pondered whether it was all a sinister trap, a scheme waiting to unfold. Did they need something scandalous to occur so they could throw in the towel? Yet, amidst the chaos, we maintained our cool, gliding through the farce with the grace of seasoned actors in a well-rehearsed drama.

Almost a week went by and the new kids still weren't there, conditioning was done now it was time for the coaches to see if they had any football players. They did this drill where you gave one guy a ball and had him lay on his back then another guy would lay on his back about three yards in front of the guy with the ball. When the coach blows the whistle both players get up as fast as they can. The one with the ball tries to get past the other guy. I think Bubba was interested in showing he was king so he chose to be the ball carrier against me. I was laughing inside which was bad but I saw this look on Coach Sovchiks face like he knew Bubba had made a mistake and he was looking at the other coaches as if to say watch this. The whistle blows and I beat him to my feet. He made the classic mistake of thinking I would stay still, but I headed straight towards him. Now, unlike that middle school kid, Bubba lowered his head. I then launched my body like a rocket, we hit head to head then he just bounced backward and man did I get an Aaaaaah. From that day forward whenever Coach wanted to introduce a new kid to the way we play he would just put them against me. It made us real tough in the end. More important than that, me and Bubba became close friends.

Going into the second week we got a busload of kids from Glenville High School. The start of a new our gang had begun. I actually consider them more like my extended family Dennis Felton, Eric Ball, Ken Mosby, Doug Mitchel, Calvin Williams and Tim Goler. Man did this team get good. The next week we got a carload full of kids from John-Hay High School. The stage was set, and I was feeling a whole lot better but you could tell they would have preferred to still be at their old school. I just kept thinking about Mr. Sampson and how badly he wanted to prove the racist haters wrong. We knew we were special and the time was now.

The team that Mr. Sampson put together went beyond that of coaches. He sought to have the most diverse staff in the county, to represent what would be the most diverse school Northeast Ohio had ever seen in its history. We were so blended that there was no majority or minority race. Inside those walls, we were one and it started on that football field.

We were not the only thing the desegregation order blended. A blend of "North American" neighborhoods was produced and I mean the neighborhoods that did not get along with each other along with "American" neighborhoods that did not like each other either. This thing was working like the perfect virus, and it was not contained; it was airborne and infecting everyone and everything. This brought in more troops for the team. As the weeks went by our two by two line of athletes got bigger and bigger. By the time school started, we were running out of equipment. Now, it was time to play. I was personally undefeated, in the three years I have played organized football. I didn't know what it felt like losing game.

Before school the first day of school we had the first game.

On the bus, the upperclassmen are talking about this school Ravenna like they were the beast of beast. This took me for a loop. It's game time and I find my edge, holding back tears, as these guys from the other team were talking shit during the warm-up and that fueled me even more. I'm gonna hurt somebody, became my number one goal while I held back my tears. First play, I smashed their back and called him a punk bitch. I was pissed. I did it again on the next two plays and they had to punt. The rest of the game it seemed like they went the other way. By the end of the game we had lost but I had 22 tackles and everyone seemed amazed. I was pissed I lost for the very first time and had never felt like that before. It's like the worst feeling in the world to me. The next game, it was more of the same and I ended up with 24 tackles. For me, this was how we played ball at Trotwood and I thought it was the way all teams played.

Time to deal with inside the school, and the rude awakening was even worse. The team of teachers was the first of its kind as this was its first day of teaching in a desegregated school and this would be the first time they would have such a diverse population. That Monday right before the bell rang to start school I saw kids running and screaming. Just like the guy that always gets killed in a horror story I run towards all the noise. In the main hallway are grown-ass white men swinging at kids. So, I go to help them and start swinging as well. Before you knew it other football players were also coming to the rescue and we eventually chased the fools out the building. They remained outside the building till the police arrived. We kept our eyes on them from the classroom windows. They were the neighborhood guys who just sat on their porches all day. They were not afraid of the police; they were all talking as if they knew each other. I have seen that before and didn't like the outcome. After about 15 minutes of that mess, we knew they were friends as no one was arrested, and they went on their way drinking on the porch.

Now, what I was not aware of was that one of the kids I helped out was named Donald William. On the street, they called him Don Juan, the leader of the Dynamite Devil gang. They were a family of guys who had to come to school by using the RTA public buses with bus tickets. For them, this was a long trip through some scary neighborhoods so they band together to stay safe. One thing led to another and they became a gang. They had to travel through the territories of the Brick City Outlaws as well as the racists on the west side.

After we didn't get any assistance from the police or our school board, Mrs. Sampson took steps in his own hands. The football players were given permission to patrol the hallways and be on alert if anyone came inside the school. The next day it happened again. This time right before lunch. On the third day, Mr. Sampson had us chain the doors closed from the inside once all students were in class. It might have seemed crazy from the outsiders' views but we were actually having fun. The connections that formed among the student body were nothing short of extraordinary—here we had Americans, North Americans, Hispanics, shades of red and brown, all standing shoulder to shoulder, united against the racists who'd dare divide us. Sometimes, this resistance even came from their own families. The virus of bigotry was alive and well, thriving in the shadows. But the teachers? They transformed into a second family, no longer just authority figures issuing directives but allies in this shared struggle. The respect that flowed between us was unprecedented, a vibrant tapestry of solidarity that I'd never witnessed before. Was fear the underlying current driving this unity? Absolutely. Those adults had every reason to be afraid, grappling with the chaos that could spill over into our space. Just imagine the juxtaposition: community members threatening harm while the kids rose up like guardians, protecting their own against the uncertainties of this new wave of students. It was a scene bursting with emotional stakes and a palpable intensity, each moment crackling with possibility.

With the chaos swirling around the school, concentration on the field became a rare commodity—like finding a clean spoon in a diner at two in the morning. Stress levels were running high, thick like fog in a noir film—players, and coaches, all racing around, just trying to avoid trouble as we sprinted to practice like we were in a high-stakes chase scene. But for me? It was a different story. The next game arrived, and I went out there like I was in a rhythm, another 21 tackles, just doing my thing. I didn't even grasp the significance of those numbers—they were mere statistics, a subplot to my main narrative—but enthusiasm surrounded me like a quirky cast of characters buzzing with excitement. Unbeknownst to me, the coaches had been trying to push me into the spotlight, nominating me for some local paper's player of the week—a title that had eluded number #15. In an attempt to stitch up the fabric between staff and students, Mr. Sampson, in a fit of camaraderie, rounded up as many teachers as he could scrape together for our next game, hoping to create some sort of peculiar community amid the inevitable absurdity.

The next game was against Maple Hts, and Jeff, the statistician and athletic trainer, took the stats and explained to me what all the hype was about regarding the stats. I guess Maple Hts took offense to all of the hype after watching us on film and was determined to shut it down. This game was different. I had never seen so many of my teachers at a game, both the middle school and high school teachers. In those days, when you made a tackle, the announcer would say your name, "and tackled by number 15 Larry Ferguson." That night I could care less about a record but I did want to hear my name all night long. It started from play one, they didn't just send the running back they gave him a lead blocker as well. On this night I really have to give some of the credit to Ken Stanback. He was a much better back than all of them.

Being able to tackle him during the week in practice made getting to these cats real easy. We were cracking heads all night and most of the time, it was for a loss and they had to give us the ball. We were close real close, and had a chance to win. Then I had the highlight hit of the year, they ran the same play as the start of the game with that lead blocker shit, I shed that block, then launched like a torpedo and cracked the running back square in his chest. In one pop, he just landed on his back and both sides of the stands went AAAAAAAAHHH. You know what that meant I did to the kid. We came up short for the win but our folks got what they came for. I ended that game with 28 tackles and a school record.

That Monday, sitting in class, the enormity of it hit me as I got the instruction to visit the local newspaper for my photo. I was the football player of the week, the "Press Star," they called it. Back then, there was no internet buzzing, no cell phones constantly lighting up, no cable shows vying for our attention. Just three television channels and those two newspapers that everyone reads. Seeing your face in print felt monumental; it was like a beacon, pointing out who to keep an eye on. With the teachers buzzing with excitement and students wrapped up in the hype, we felt like rock stars, bathed in a glow of adoration. It was a time when guys from "North America" dated girls from "America," and vice versa. It wasn't about color; everyone was just flowing together, and it was a beautiful chaos. The "D.E.A.D"s had lost this round, and the chance of cashing in on that metaphorical bad check Dr. King spoke of felt tangible—a glimmer of possibility for the future. Yet, lurking just beyond the horizon was another adversary, a historical one that needed confronting, waiting silently, prepared to shake up our newfound harmony.

The bulk of our kids came from a very strong and proud community. Most of their parents, aunts, uncles, brothers and sisters had attended that local school and they were expected to do the same. Their families were Tarblooders bleeding black through and through. They actually began building the school the year I was born 1965. A Tarblooder was the Glenville mascot, which was a robot man who didn't bleed red but bled black tar from working on the railroads. This was the historical Glenville High School with a rich heritage that includes the creators of Superman, politicians like Howard Metzenbaum, entertainer Steve Harvey and Major Michael White. They were synonymous with winning the State of Ohio Track and Field title more than any school in the history of the state and its Coach Robert Bump Taylor who led them to titles in 73' 74' and 75' was still there just waiting on his next generation. They didn't just belong to Cleveland Tarblooders belonging to the State of Ohio.

Now, the kids that were bused were no longer Tarblooder but became Wolverines at Lincoln-West High School on the west side of Cleveland and the future looked bleak, so many thought. At Glenville, the coaches knew the kids they needed to field good sports teams so without complaints they protected them from being bused. On the football side, the brother combinations of Kevin Shorts and Cecil Short were the quarterback and receiver respectively speaking. Kevin is arguably one of the best quarterbacks that I have seen play on any level just never got the shot. Cecil's son, Cecil III. benefited from the struggles of his uncle and dad. Cecil III. went on to star in the NFL. The brother combination of Tracy Haynes and Terrance Haynes was the running and defensive stall wards that they needed. After that everyone else was expendable. This was something I took offense to and made sure my cats understood the Tarblooders were enemy number one. But getting the guys to part ways with family was really difficult. In many ways on the field against Glenville was a civil war. To this end "The D.E.A.D" had gotten a shot off but we were determined to not let that kill us.

I had been sidelined with a finger injury that occurred in practice after the Maple Hts game. It wasn't that bad, the middle finger on my throwing hand just came off splitting into two pieces at the knuckle. Funny, there wasn't a lot of blood, just two white bones sticking out. After forging some doctors' notes and a soft cast I was clear to play and now it was time. I had come up with some chants to bond and hype my teammates, and it took off like wildfire. It was a nice call and response with them just saying yeah, that went like this, Me "I got that feelin'" "YeaH" "we gonna kick some ass" "YeaH" "I got that feelin'" "YeaH" "Kevin Shorts won't pass" "Yeah" "I got that feelin'" "Yeah" "we number one" "Yeah" "I got that feelin'" "Yeah" "them bums gonna run" "YEAH... The greatest bond was that we all "American" and "North American" began to pray together regardless of our beliefs. I would hear folks say football builds character. For us football brought out the character of this blended bunch of desegregated kids. We were Champions.

The truth of the matter was Glenville was good, they really were stacked and Kevin Shorts was no joke but I had to find a way to make him the enemy and this chant worked. It was a great game hard fought. I made a touchdown-saving tackle against the Haynes boy and we were able to hold on for the win and shocked everyone. This win did it and everyone was all in for the next three years. Students, teachers, band, cheerleaders, basketball you name it they were in. They were no longer Tarblooder, they were Wolverines who could walk on the eastside and westside holding their heads high. My sister was a senior that year, and I felt the proudest for her, she could see I really wasn't that bad. For some reason, I felt bad for Glennville. This was a historic "North American" community that appeared to be stripped of its greatness through the loss of its children. Man, how great could we have been if we were one instead of being split? After the season the team voted Bubba the MVP. He had endured a lot of defeat at Lincoln-West his entire time there and it was great seeing him go out a winner. He is now an Officer for the Cleveland Fire Department.

TIME TO EXHALE

Let's really sit with the implications of my circumstance during that key moment, shall we? There's a strange irony in the fervent opposition to the civil rights movement—the players in what I'd liken to a grim shadow-puppet show, the ones I've dubbed the D.E.A.D.S. These antagonists, a veritable army of stubbornness, wield a disconcerting amount of power. Sure, I managed to find an ally, a flicker of hope in an otherwise bleak landscape of injustice, but I was also grappling with the insidious allure of my own inner demons. These temptations turned me into a labyrinthine figure, a potential menace not just to society's broader canvas, but especially to the very fabric of my own community and the women in it. It's an unpalatable reality, this shadow of truth, but it's crucial to confront it if we want to even think about progressing.

In the rawest essence of my being, I was a creature untamed, devoid of the refinement that society demands. At 15 years old, I was thrust into a world where the burdens of manhood fell upon me, and yet I roamed like a beast. My body, a testament to my youth, was now capable of creation with but the slightest act, yet I remained blind to the responsibilities accompanying such power. Grooming was a foreign concept; I bore the unkempt signs of my existence—hair sprouting defiantly beneath my chin, the scent of musk marking my armpits, and my meager wardrobe reduced to just three pairs of undergarments and filthy socks. My front teeth were a testament to neglect, while my hair, a chaotic, uncut mane, stood as a crown of wildness. I lived a transient life, like a drifter with no abode, merely crashing on friends' couches in basements, sprawled out on attic floors, and seeking respite on porches. The purpose of school eluded me; I sat through standardized tests oblivious to their significance, resorting to random guesses, for I couldn't even recall their names. The concept of driving was alien, dreams of a car or a home were mere shadows on the periphery of my consciousness, and comfortable belongings felt as distant as the stars. What was I to seek in a companion? Should it merely be her affirmation of affection for me? I grappled with this confusion, struggling to articulate my feelings. And emotions? They swirled within me like a tempest—jealousy, sadness, joy, anger, frustration, anxiety, shame, love, lust, empathy, and envy—all foreign entities I lacked the means to comprehend. Reflecting upon those tumultuous days, I see clearer now: there was no guide, no mentor to illuminate the path ahead. I was simply a creature of nature, navigating my own wild course as so many untrained animals do. in the tapestry of life, we often find ourselves weaving threads of pain and regret, not only for our own experiences but for those we touch unwittingly with our actions. It is a heavy burden to acknowledge that my ignorance of what it means to embody manhood became a source of suffering for others. Like a bullet, I inadvertently struck those around me, leaving wounds that may still linger in the hearts of many. This state of being—my emotional tumult—was not a mere twist of fate; it was a manifestation of the very circumstances that shaped my existence. I was, in many ways, the portrait that society wished to paint, a child reared without the guiding hand of a father, lost in a world where I was called to become something greater. I carry within me the names of those who felt the ripple effects of my unawareness, each enduring their own burdens due to my struggles. To them, I extend my heartfelt apologies, recognizing the pain that my journey has inflicted upon their lives. Yet, it is crucial to note that amidst the chaos within, there resided an indomitable spirit—a belief in my own worth and potential. Though the world may have seen me as incomplete, I recognized the nobility that dwelled within me. This resilience defined my character, allowing moments of connection even as I navigated toward emotional collapse. The legacy of pain I caused is but a small fraction when measured against the profound injustices faced by many in this ongoing struggle for civil rights. My mother, a beacon of hope and strength, tirelessly endeavored to shield me from harm and despair, and through her unwavering prayers and sacrifices, we sought a brighter path. Today, I stand before you, acknowledging my past, aspiring to grow, and committed to fostering healing, for it is through understanding our shared humanity that we can forge a future rich in compassion and equity.

In a surprise move over Christmas break, my mother moved again. The new crib was even further west. It was like she was trying to find a Trotwood in Cleveland. The home was located in the last neighborhood before the airport and Berea, Ohio. We were nowhere close to Lincoln-West. It was my sister's senior year and she only had five(5) months of school left so it didn't make any sense to change her school. This meant she would have to take public transportation to school by herself and that wasn't happening. So, I gotta stay a Wolverine for the moment she said.

I could tell something else was going on though because mamma was getting these paranoid looks again and made sure we kept the doors locked and curtains closed. About nine months before we had left Townview we had a life-altering incident. One night while we were asleep, some white drug addicts had crawled through the family room window. They must have been in the house for a while based on the findings. I remember my mother yelling out my name frantically, "Junie, Junie, JUNIE. I slept on the top bunk in our room and immediately flopped down. Then I saw it, someone dashing right past my doorway. By reflex, I took off after them. I could hear Mamma still yelling my name as I chased them out the back door. I could tell it was two of them by the time I got to the kitchen. It was dark so I didn't follow them out to the backyard fence. I ended up stopping right in front of our television. They had been in the house long enough to have piled up our valuables in the backyard. Mamma had a habit of sleeping with her purse by the bed. When the asshole tried to get to her purse, it woke her and that's when she began to scream. Funny thing was I was the only person she screamed for. When the police arrived, she was still shook up and had that paranoid look on her face. These same assholes were bold and for the next couple of days watched her from across the street as she would get out the car to come in the house from work. A friend of hers loaned us a dog and she got a pistol from somewhere. A couple of days, they tried to grow some balls. I was watching her get out of the car and when I went to open the door for her we both saw them coming across the street. I guess they thought they could get to her before she got to the door. I quickly let her in and slammed the door shut locking it real quick. That didn't stop them, though. They had gotten their own dog and were banging on the door. Now, at this point, I wanted to open the door and just get it on. Mamma was on the phone with the pigs. Then she reached for this bible and pulled out the gun. I was super hyped, time to kill these stupid mutha fuckers. But she was shaking and sat down. Me, I wasn't scared; I was pissed. I had developed a numbness to racist at that point and I was only 13 years old. Now, it's been about 15 minutes and these fools are still cursing, "fuck you, you mother fucking Nigger" "coon bitch open the damn door" while beating on the door. I was like, "Let me shoot them through the window." Then she put the gun away. I was so disappointed. The pigs arrived while the guys were still at the crib. It was three of them and they talked for about five minutes. Then one was placed in the car and the other two went on their way. I can remember two things changing after that day. The first was Mamma stopped smoking those funny-smelling cigarettes and secondly, that was the last time I saw that look on her face until now. This look told me she was running away from Tremont, so I was cool with everything because I knew she was running from D.E.A.D.s. We moved out of the district to a home a few blocks from the airport. Now, how would I get to school?

HEART OF A CHAMPION

I am approaching my 22nd straight month in school. Mr. Sampson can see that tired look on my face again. We haven't had any talks in a while and there was this new kid who just arrived from the Dominican Republic, a baseball player named Louis Martinez. Mr. Sampson thought it might be cool if I helped him get adjusted since we were both on that side of town. I let Mr. Sampson know I had no problem with helping but I had moved and was scared to tell anyone that I was out of the district. Man, he got this look on his face then looked left and right and as quick as he appeared it was gone. He then asked if I wanted to stay, and I assured him I did but I don't know if I can keep taking the train because my mamma has been complaining about money lately. He then sent me off to class. That very same day, mamma tells us that my sister Bonita is pregnant. Now, this was puzzling to me because I made sure no one at the school hit it, so how did she get pregnant? We'll come to find out my aunt Linda set Bonita up on a prom date with this guy that attends her church, Anthony Bryant was his name. Sis done fell for the okey-doke and gave up the panties with no protection. How can they be a family when they only knew each other for a week? The "D.E.A.D"s just shot them both with temptation. Now, the first thing that came to mind was to whoop his ass, one for my sis and two because I know we won't have enough money for me to stay at the school. But I said I would chill as long as he treated her right. Man, I held that promise to myself for about 10 years but that's another story.

The week before school ended I was called to the guidance office. Mr. Sampson had spoken to my counselor about my problem and put together a plan to take care of everything. In those days the school systems had a summer work program for the underprivileged. They had set it up so that I would have a job for the next two months at the local rec center. The school was also given public transportation bus tickets for the students who lived in areas that were too sparse to get school buses. Every week I would get my stipend of those so that I could get back and forth. It was all a go still the first day of work. This is 1981 in the city of Cleveland which just happens to be a very liberating time for the gay community. The rec location was at the bathhouse. Now, I did not know what a bathhouse was until a guy at my uncle's barbershop explained it to me. He said it's called a bathhouse because people go there to get in the water and they get in the water together. He told me to check to see if they have showers and stuff and then you will know. Now, I am in the chair getting a cut so I am trying to be still. Uncle's not saying anything so I thought maybe this cat was on to something. So I asked him, "What's wrong with taking a shower we do it after practice all the time." He then responded, "Yeah but do your teammates wash your dick or do you do it? In the bath house strangers will do it for you," Then I got it.

The first day at work, I went looking for water and sure enough there was somewhere to bathe. It was on Starkweather right across from the swimming pool. Man, what have I gotten into? Safe to say the first day did not happen. They called home as I was a no-show, and I said I could not find the place. I was told to just go to the pool. The next day I found out that the pool area was my assignment and they just used some office space in that building called the Bath House, which just so happens to have places in it where people could actually take a bath. Twenty years later I learned I may have been safer at the bathhouse than at the pool.

Most of the kids that came to the park and pool knew I was a ball player at the high school. This was sort of cool because most of them were Hispanic and only played at the park. We did play a lot of dominoes though. Anyway, a recent grad of Lincoln-West would always chill with us at Lincoln Park as it was the only piece of greenery in the area. I remember him well because he was proud to have been a graduate of the school and I was its quarterback. He and his family lived in the area for a while he stayed around the corner from the junior high school and down the street from the hostess bakery spot that was there back then. He would bring extra ho hos they would take from the trucks when no one was watching. He had the same last name that the school was on his name was Ariel Castro.

In 2002 this fool done up and kidnapped three girls and kept them in his house for 11 years. He even got one of them pregnant and delivered the baby in the house. I drove my kids to his crib the last time I was in Cleveland but they had torn it down. They made a movie after this cat called "The Cleveland Kidnappings". But that's another story. The summer gig went good, I was hoping not spending any money on me would make it easier for my mother to take care of Bonita. The new guy Louie was also at the park with me every day and we would get the chance to workout before the season. The "D.E.A.D"s had shot my sister but I was still able to do my thing thanks to Mr. Sampson.

When the first day of practice starts it's night and day from last year. Everyone is there and then some. This group was more athletic than anything else and this sort created a bind for me. We had no one poised enough to run the offense so I ended up as the starting quarterback. What they did not know was after the injury to my finger last year I had lost feeling in that area and was having a hard time throwing the ball. I could command the offense but passing was no longer a strong point. But I was happy as long as I got to hit people. We also picked up two new black coaches, for which I am sure Mr. Sampson had something to do with. Things were evolving that most were not anticipating, especially those who opposed civil rights. Desegregation was making us innovators culturally. Our cheerleaders, the band, teachers, bus drivers we were all not looking to assimilate to a white society; we were out to make a whole new one for ourselves. Most didn't understand that any attack on a "North American" person would bring just as much harm to the American person we were in-tangled with, We were vested in each other. This was often validated in the open dialogue we would have with each other.

For some the truth was sad, and those were normally the American folks when that rude awakening of their institutionalized racism would conflict with the truth they now knew from their own experiences with someone different. This innovation was so freeing, we took things beyond color and found ourselves representing everyone who just wanted the freedoms afforded to them as people, including gays the handicaps and various religions. We didn't let anyone mess with anyone. Shit one of our coaches Jeff was gay. we knew it and we didn't care, our volleyball coach was gay we didn't care, our P.E. teacher was gay we didn't care and it made us all stronger. This had also begun to infect the community around the school. There were no more attacks now we could really get back to education

The season got off to a slow start primarily due to me. The schedule was tougher but we should have still done better. I was once again in the sights of the D.E.A.D.'s gun. I was the quarterback and having team chemistry was important so I rarely went home after practice. Most of the guys lived in the Glenville neighborhoods between East 105th and St. Clair and East 106th and Superior. This covered two gang areas that were dominated by the Dynamite Devils. Because of this, a minimum of four days out of the week, I would fall asleep at a teammate's house. There were three guys who really looked out for me: Dennis Felton and upperclassmen Eric Ball and Ken Mosby. They always had somewhere for me to sleep and a little something to eat with no questions asked. It didn't hurt that I was a girl magnet either. No, all jokes aside, most girls in those days always had a girlfriend with them and I was good at making it easy so my boys could be one-on-one with their girl.

There was one girl in particular though, her name was

Miranda Hamilton. She was primarily with Eric; but was real close friends with Dennis, Bubba, Calvin and later on Tim. Miranda just happened to be one of the captains on the cheerleader squad so her crib was the hangout. She kept some girls around and that was cool with me. I think I had given girls a false sense of who I really was because I was from the west side. This made it easy for them to sample me. This was really new to me as I still believed that it should be one person for the rest of my life. But I am starting to think that's a dream and just doesn't happen. It was clean fun, though and for some reason, I always checked with her to see if a chick was cool enough for me. This was the new "Our Gang", and they gave me permission to lead them on the field.

One day this new cheerleader that I tried to get to know during last school year, approached me. Now, I consider myself to be one who does not go back and forth and this young lady had chosen to date another guy instead of me and I was cool with that. She asked if I would escort her to her debutante ball. First, thing that came to my mind was that she realized she made a mistake and now she wanted me. So, I asked, "What about your boyfriend?" Then she replies, " he's ok with it." Now, I am taken for a loop, this was a first, these cats here are cool with another dude taking their girl out. Come to find out she was being raised by her father a superfly type of dude and had an aunt who was trying to help out. That's them pictured above. So, I said cool. For the next couple of weeks I went to these rehearsals to learn how to waltz, 123, 123, it was nice. We even went over the proper way to sit and eat. For some reason, most of that was natural to me. Now, all the other guys and girls there were couples but me and Tonya were not. Oh yeah her name was Tonya Owens, a very pretty redbone.

Anyway, I promised myself I would respect her boyfriend at all costs but people really didn't believe we were just schoolmates. Man, I could have used some fatherly advice on this one. I had very little money left from the Bath House gig and I had to pay for a tuxedo. Why am I spending money on a girl that belongs to someone else? What kind of sucker am I? It just so happened that our pre-season scrimmage was against Warrensville Hts, High School which was within walking distance to the Holiday Inn, at Randal Park Mall which was where the Ball was being held the same night. Now, I am in this all by myself, no help from mom, pops, uncle or aunt. I am really faking the funk, guess I am preserving some image.

That morning I didn't ride the school bus to Warrensville with the team. I used my school bus tickets and hauled my football pads and tux stuff to the Hotel. I then hustled over to the field which was about two blocks away. When I got there they had already started and Coach Sovchik was pissed. I really wasn't being bad, it just happened. During the scrimmage, a guy slams into my right knee and it just buckles. The pain was bad. I could still move but I was not myself for sure. I went back in for a couple of series, really being careful then the day was over. Because I had hurt myself, I was told to ride the bus back to school. This made it even worse, because now I had to use more bus tickets to get back out to Warrensville to the Ball. The D.E.A.D.s are kicking my ass right now. My patients are really short, I am just worried about being able to Walz in the tux as a favor for someone else's girls. Needless to say, I got there on time and was able to dance but I was in pain. The girl's parents had arranged hotel rooms for the guys as a thank you measure as well as a changing room. The next day everyone was going to Cedar Point as couples. Me I had had it, I was in pain, and just wanted to lie down, plus I was broke. I was in a one-parent household that had a grown child in the house that had a baby on the way. I was maxed out. Then it got worse, and they all started drinking including Tonya, several of them would come to my room and ask me to please come to Cedar Point and I just couldn't get it. I could hear them parting the rest of the night.

The next morning I just got up and went home. Till today, I have never spoken to Tonya about all of that. This was the second time I had experienced that odd sense of loyalty. The first time was with a friend of hers for whom I was brave enough to meet her family mom included in an effort to show how interested I really was in her. She had a cool family: two older brothers, the Patton brothers. I thought that might be cool. Alicia Patton was her name then out of nowhere one day she's up and dating a teammate of mind Forrest Sanders. That one hurt for a while and side effects still linger today but we will address that later.

That Monday they checked my knee to make sure I could practice then before we lined up two by two; Coach Sovchik called me into his office. He goes on to tell me how disappointed he was in me for what happened and that his quarterback has to lead by example. By this time I was really over it because I knew what my intentions were. The "D.E.A.D"s have me in their sights again. Up to this point, I have always respected Mr. Sovcik, but his institutionalized racism was kicking in and really clouded his awareness of the actions he was about to take. He told me to bend over and take these three swats for being late. I really don't think he or others understand the origin behind inflicting pain on a "North American" person by an "American" person via their physical efforts by means of a paddle, billy club or whip. Both parties are now being taken back in time. In this case, 300 years. The message sent is; boy do as you are told, or I will hurt you. This fool did not get it and proceeded to hit me with that flat wooden stick of his three times. What could have stopped these past three days of misunderstandings? I just put it past me as the show must go on.

By the fourth game, it was apparent that something had to change and it came from an unexpected person. My coach Mr. Brady had been watching closely, especially during the pre-games and finally reached a conclusion he could no longer hold back. I was the hype for the team and especially for those who were scared to go to battle. I had learned some years back how to get my adrenaline flowing so tough I would be fighting back tears. This was how I got my edge. He told me to stop. In a calm, cool manner, he was like, "We need you to lead us, but if you can't see then you're going to walk us into a wall." You make yourself so mad at the start of the game to the point you are crying. That may be good for a linebacker but it's poison for a QB. You just have to be cool." From that day forward not only was I cool I was downright cold as ice. He was right, once I did that I was able to really command the offense and we went on a winning streak. The bad side of this was at 5'9" I was small for a quarterback and I could not play QB at the next level. In the long run, I truly believe it saved my life because I was playing the game in the most dangerous fashion possible. There wasn't a single game that went by when I didn't knock myself out. Sometimes they wouldn't know, other times they would put some smelling salt under my nose and send me right back into the game. Today two of the guys I learned to play that way with in Trotwood have either broken their necks and are paralyzed (Mike Stankovich) or have serious brain problems to the extent they have nearly lost their life (Donny Sizer). Guys keep fighting, as you are always in our prayers.

I turned into this Iceberg just in time. Once the neighborhood racists ceased from attacking the kids at the school, the gangs turned their attention to the students. There was this California gang explosion going on with crips and blood and our local gangs were choosing which one to be affiliated with and began to recruit real heavy in the school. Now, we were having gang fight after gang fight and walking the street, and catching the bus or train on either side of town was getting dangerous. For some odd reason, the number of buses the school district was using to transport the high school students across town decreased by over 50% and they just gave students bus tickets. On a weekly basis, those kids would all meet in the center of town at the Tower City building to change either buses or trains. What a recipe for disaster. On a weekly basis fights between them would break out and it seemed like the adults were happy about it. The newspaper writers would get there just before the students in anticipation of the action but the cops wouldn't show up till later. It was like they wanted to kill each other. Luckily the results were mere bumps and bruises. This made our team even closer as we would check on each other and know one went anywhere in town by themselves.

We formed a buddy system and I ended up with a new buddy named Tim Goler. He was an underclassman who couldn't wait to be a Wolverine. He said he would do anything the team needed and meant it. He just wanted to get on the field. We needed someone who could snap my football and that became Tim. He was center, Dennis was my back, and Calvin was my number one receiver. We felt unstoppable other guys were key contributors as this was a total team in all spots. Now, we are in the game that would finally make us Senate champs. It was Civil War II against the Tarblooders. We were really confident in our running game, the question was could we hold off Kevin Shorts and their passing game so I went back to defense but not as a linebacker but as a safety in our prevent defensive scheme. It shook them up again. This time we just took it to them for the win. We are the North Senate champions and will now be playing on TV for the whole marbles.

Now, since we've been back in Cleveland, I have not seen pops. I've been busy and really didn't notice it that much. This is a cquarterback. This meant the other team would get film on us to determine championship week and it triggered an unexpected string of events. John F. Kennedy was the school we were going to play. For me, it was like something out of the movies because during that era we only had three stations and they only played 11 games on TV for the whole year and this was one. I was the starting how to win the game. When Kennedy showed their team the scouting film on us there I was. My cousin James Ferguson was one of the star defensive players. We now have another Civil War game. Jamie was a cousin from my Pops' side of the family he was cool as ice as well. I was more like that side of the family than my siblings. Our grandfather came here from the Bahamas and we kept that heritage alive. It was an acknowledgment that we weren't total descendants of slaves. It made the family feel proud knowing they had two of us going at it. Then there he is before the game, I get to see Pops. I was happy to see him and after we hugged, I wanted everyone in the place to hear Ferguson all night.

When I got back in the locker room I saw something I had not seen since that first bus ride on my very first game as a Wolverine. Cats were looking scared, with the exception of a couple of dudes. I couldn't get over hyped but something wasn't right. The game starts and I return the kickoff to start the game. We were a running team, which meant the offensive line had to perform. The first three runs the crowd heard Ferguson, Ferguson, Ferguson, but it wasn't for me it was for Jamie. The next time we got the ball, they heard Ferguson, Ferguson, it was me. It went on like that the entire first half. We were losing by two touchdowns at the half. When we got to the locker room I saw something for the very first time. Some cats were yelling at each other then some were asking each other, "You got some more?" They began to hand each other these pills. I whispered, "What the hell is that?" Someone replied, "some speed, I didn't know if the truth. I looked in amazement and walked away. I did my routine to get this thing turned around and ran out for the second half. We came out the gate in the second half with a Ferguson run, Ferguson run, Purifoy touchdown. After that touchdown, the team acted as if we had won the game. As long as we didn't get blanked, they were happy but I was pissed. I could tell the coaches knew something was up because they drew up a new offense during the game. They put me in the shot gut and had Tim snap me the ball and I would run left or right. Today they call it the "WildCat" That really created a Ferguson, Ferguson, Ferguson for the rest of the night. Today they call that the wildcat. Needless to say, we lost the game, but the night was far from over. Looking back on it, I feel sad. That day I had the men in my family finally there all as one. Just knowing they were there brought enough support for me to be who I was.

THE ORGY AND BUMP

The night of that final game in 82' the cheerleaders had organized a viewing party of the game at Miranda's house. What started as a simple group of kids who just wanted to watch themselves on TV got wild. Before you knew it, there had to be almost 60 people in the house from the basement to the top floor. Me, I am still pissed and still had my uniform on. I was not much of a drinker and the gang knew. Some might say I invented the cooler because the only way I could even taste beer was if it had some 7up in it. That night, they were all there, though, and I mean the girls. But I wanted the radio. You see, on this same night, my first "Our Gang" was in the State playoff game against Keith. Trotwood Madison vs. Dayton Roth. By this time, Keith was the number one ranked back in the state. He had become unstoppable and was going to attend Ohio State. For me, It was another Civil War and I wanted to hear as much of it as I could on an am station.

It was just as emotional for me to listen to that game and hear the call out Sistrunk, Byers, Douglas, Jones, Crosby, Daniels, and Sizer as it was hearing Ferguson. It was a replay but in those days, there was no way to get the final score without having talked to someone at the game. The more I listened to that game, the lonelier I began to feel. It had gotten so crowded that the only spot I could find that no one else wanted was on top of the backrest of a couch. I had my headphones on trying to listen and they were going at. Then on a commercial break, I would look over at folks having fun like we won the Super Bowl. It was then that I knew I was as different as Mr. Sampson said I was.

The question was no longer what I was doing but what I had done. Trotwood had won. I fell asleep amidst the noise, the laughter, the wildness of it all. Somehow, I found myself balanced on the backrest of a couch, sleep claiming me soundly. When I opened my eyes, I saw her there—an Angel on the couch beneath me. The night had passed without any disturbance as if she had guarded my slumber. Others were sprawled out in disarray, but she remained serene in her repose. I studied her, and the longer I looked, the more I began to think she might be the one meant for me. It was a thought both thrilling and frightening. I resolved to leave before the others stirred. But as I rolled to rise, I found us face to face.

There was an urge to kiss her, but uncertainty held me. I chose instead to awaken her gently. "Excuse me," I murmured, breaking the silence that had wrapped around us. Her expression tempted me to stay, to linger. Her name was Robin Griggs—a friend, a cousin to Sheryl Miranda's friend. She was not from their world, and perhaps that was what I needed. But for now, the moment had to pass. I slipped out through the back door. That was to be my last night with them like that. I saw them one final time at the banquet, a blur of faces and laughter. It flooded me with joy to see Calvin Williams of "Our Gang II" claiming the MVP trophy. Later, he would rise to become Chief of Police in Cleveland, a testament to his spirit and strength.

The folks that were really fighting against integrating were starting to fight back. This put added pressure on Mr. Sampson. Our victories against Glenville did serve a notice and one particular person took action on it. The legendary Glenville track coach Robert Bump Taylor transferred to Lincoln-West. Now, this guy is a three-time state champion and could go anywhere he wanted but he chose to be a Wolverine. Don't get it twisted. He knew we had talent there but we needed a "North American" teacher. Not just the "North American" kids but the All kids too.

Let me be clear: the psychological effects of this challenge are more daunting than the task of integrating our children. After the impact of Coach Sovcik's paddling, I found a silver lining that I hadn't expected. Now, I want to speak directly to my fellow Americans, especially those who have navigated the world as white Americans. I appreciate you. However, let us take a moment to reflect: for the vast majority of your educational journey, from the time you enter school to our civil rights milestones, the predominant face and voice you encounter is that of another white American. Education, my friends, is not just a topic for debate; it's a curriculum steeped in truth. When the narratives you hear come solely from white American mouths, a powerful notion takes root—one that suggests that these voices represent the truth. For eleven consecutive decades, what else can the human mind conclude but that white Americans are the keepers of truth? As a North American man, I acknowledge something significant: my greatest adversary is often perceived to be the white American male. Yet, we must recognize the reality that for a major portion of our population, it's nearly impossible to flip this script.

Many white Americans across this vast landscape can count their North American teachers on one hand, if that. And those students who lack diversity in their educational experiences find themselves at a grave disadvantage. Had desegregation not broken this cycle, I might have unconsciously been programmed to favor the views of one American leader over another, simply based on their shared identity. However, this paradigm shifted with the arrival of my first North American male teacher, Robert Bump Taylor. Now, when I raise this point, many will instinctively offer a counterargument that seeks to dismiss the complexities of our reality. You might hear them say, "Why can't we trust all teachers equally?" This belief, while well-meaning, often lacks context.

We live in a society of beautiful diversity—we look different, we are different—and that is not just acceptable; it is essential. The power of choice belongs to every heartbeat that graces this earth. A North American man embodies a different essence from that of a white American man. When given equal exposure, each option enriches our understanding and enables us to make more informed choices. This was something I was taught by Bump. He promised that "American" (white) folks would become stronger as well just because we are integrated and he was right. He made sure I understood that there are those out there who are willing to lose a thousand of their own just to stop one of you. "North American" folks are fighting for those thousands as well. Man, was he a fortune teller, as that's exactly what happened.

After the season, there wasn't a reason to go to the East Side that much, so I found myself talking on the phone more than going through that transportation hustle. Plus, it was starting to get dangerous out there for me. It's basketball season and at most games, I am still the hype guy. We just came off winning the football senate title and now we wanted to move and had a loaded basketball team to do it as well. The title was coming down to us and John Hay High School. I had a classmate, Hilene Rainey, who was one of our girls' best players and was dating some guy on Hay's team named Charles

Oakley, a future NBA enforcer. Man, they would give her the business and on this day, they gave us a bus just for our students to go to the game as well but she didn't want to go. We needed as many folks or big mouths as possible so I talked her into coming but once there, she was back and forth. She knew Hay was not just going to take that ass beating quietly.

My dumb as had this chick that went to Hay, but her father had a funeral home in Glenville on 105th Street called Strowders. I was determined to get that pickle wet and figured I would just go to her crib instead of getting on the bus. During half-time, we walked outside and began to walk across their football practice field to her crib. I had just got a letterman's jacket, red, white and blue with Lincoln-West on it, big as day. When we got halfway across the field, two dudes ran up on me, swinging hand like crazy. Clearly soft as mother fuckers as they both ran when I got a lucky lick in.

Nonetheless, I ended up going back into the game, which had a few minutes left. When the game ended we lined up with the team and started heading to the bus. Sure enough, the minute we step outside the school to get on the bus, a mob of cats start coming at us with everything. They didn't care about girls or not. They were just trying to get some shots in. It was the DDs, Dynamite Devil gang as they called themselves. I was helping as many people get on the bus as possible. The bus driver was in a panic. No school officials were there. They had lined up in a gauntlet, ready to throw rocks at the bus. This thing was a mess. Girls were just crying then the bus driver couldn't get the door closed of all things. A dude tried to come onto the to throw something and I caught his ass right at the first step. The bus is moving slow but she can't close the door and me and this cat are going at it. She is finally able to close the door but I still got his whole arm inside and was trying to break off. She had a butter knife the cuzin to the one I had when I was in the 3rd grade in her cup holder. I was able to grab it and was swinging to his chest, and just in a nick of time, she opened the door and he fell out. Man, I was saved again from taking someone's life. There had to be something else going on that was part of their history that I didn't know about. But I got to start going home no matter the situation. It was after that that Bump took me aside and had our mentoring talk.

I went back to just chillin' on the phone. Most of the time it was with a particular classmate, Nellie Lewis, that I said was off limits because she had dated my partner Dennis at one time in middle school. After weeks of talking, she assured me that what was between her and Dennis was not a serious thing; it was just middle school infatuation that flared up in high school some years later. The emotions were high but I was determined not to step where my boy had been. I mean, if I had to, I would have killed someone for Dennis. I loved the guy. She had also been friends with a young lady whom I dated briefly, named Angela, so this was a real bad look. Man, o Man, do I need someone to help me right now, because I am really about to get in "D.E.A.D"'s sits again.

I finally got the nerve to go to her crib. It was cool, we were just friends. She had a little brother named John John, and he was trying to do his homework. I remember it just like it was yesterday, it was a clock worksheet he was learning how to tell time. I think I spent more time with him than I did with her. The next couple of times, they taught me how to play this game called Frogger on an Atari machine. Then, on that third visit, it just happened. I felt something I had never felt before and could not fight it off. I find myself having to pause right now as I am writing about it just thinking about it. I guess I am too emotional for my own good. We were having a friendly dispute over a game of Frogger. How the story goes is somehow, we were face to face just when I am putting on my shoes to leave, and without hesitation, we kissed and my heart was growing. Not dropping but growing bigger and bigger for every second we were kissing. I went out the door in a daze. Instead of getting on the bus to Tower City, I walked 99 blocks down St. Clair to the Tower City train station.

The entire walk I am on an emotional roller coaster. I had tried my hardest not to let this happen, so my rationale was that this was bigger than me. Dennis was my friend, so I felt it best to tell him before it got around school. So I sent word through who? Yep, Miranda. All I wanted to do was have her tell him I would be in the gym second period. Do you know before the first period was over, the word on the street was that Felton and Ferguson were going to fight 2nd period in the gym? The only thing I could do was control myself and I had decided that if it came down to fighting, I would just let him hurt me. I'm not laying a finger on him. Man, when we saw all those folks, we just went the other way and talked about it. He was really into the integration thing going on at school. Just finished dating an "American" white girl and was really digging this Hispanic chic. Till today, I still don't think he knew how real my emotions were for her but that's cool. The best thing about this relationship was it got me focused on grades as I was really thinking about the future, and I mean the future as an adult.

Just when I thought I was breaking through, that's when I really needed a clear head or a "pops" the most. Man, I'm lost in it—she got my heart flipping and right when I feel like it can't take another hit, here comes the curveball. Ania, her stepmother, she pulls us aside and hits us with it, plain as day, "Yo, y'all planning to have sex?" And before I could even stutter, she's like, "Yes." I'm frozen, mind racing. I mean, I know at that age it's all about the chase, that thrill. But deep down, I was just about the vibes with her, wanting those good moments. Then her mom drops the bomb, saying she'll set her up for the pill. And I'm over the moon. I got a love on my side, her fam's on my team, and everything's lining up just right. The rest of that school year? Man, it felt like a dream. Track wasn't even my main gig. I was more like an intern to Bump, learning the ropes and soaking in the game. Track let me roll with the homies from Dayton, traveling the state, chasing that competition, seeing how they grew from boys to men. The real highlight was those deep talks about our next moves in life, got me reflecting hard. I started pulling away from those who didn't share that vision, caught in that tension between two worlds. This new love? It amplified everything and made me question where I stood.

A LIFE TAKEN

I was in love. I really took committing to someone seriously. Maybe it was due to witnessing the relationships my mother had and learning what not to do. This one also made me have to mature. But this was difficult as I was missing a whole lot of tools. If I had to count, I would say I slept at Nell's house four days a week. It was rather convenient for everyone. Her mother worked in nursing and was consistently gone till 5:00 a.m. Her father was a cool dude who loved to bowl and did this at least five days a week. The bowling alley didn't close till 4, so he would be home just before 5:00 a.m. Now, out of respect, I always left the house before they got home, but for a high school kid, what a life. Funny thing is most would have thought it was about two horny teenagers and sex. That wasn't the case for me. It was about all of us: me, her, her mother, father, uncle, sisters, nephews, and even her sister's boyfriends. I just loved the whole unit of things, so I didn't want to cloud it with just sex. I needed a family. That's what I thirst for as the "D.E.A.D"s had divided mine.

It's now summertime; I finally get a break. It's a little more difficult to get to Nellie's house as bus tickets were now slim, and Mamma messed up my summer gig. She didn't understand why they had given me the ok for the summer job program but not my brother. I kept trying to explain to her to just leave it alone. My school did it for me. But when they realized someone else might find out, I was out. I was pissed. By the time I got to the Eastside to see my girl, it had been over a week. We talked on the phone, but it was not the same. Then, I experienced a new emotion. Her dad was a cool dude and had been for years. Actually, I am surprised he is not somehow related to me. Nell's mothers and her sister lived upstairs, and Nellie, along with her stepmother and stepbrother, lived downstairs, and he made sure everyone got along. When the summer break hit, he introduced my girl to a brother she did not know she had also named John. He was cool and lived in a suburb about 30 minutes away.

For nearly six months, I had occupied Nellie's sacred space —those evenings now belonged to me, and in those moments, I felt an overwhelming sense of euphoria. However, that state was ephemeral (which means over); now, all I could perceive was a new presence: Johnny. Jealousy, an unfamiliar and unwelcome emotion, emerged within me, and I was ill-equipped to comprehend its nature or tame it. In my ignorance, I adopted the persona of the irate man. This strategy yielded no fruit; before long, I rashly declared it was over—an insincere proclamation spurred by a tempest of emotion—as I stormed away. Stubbornness soon took residence in me, compelling me to maintain my distance for over a week. In retrospect, I have often labeled that period as one of my gravest errors. Indeed, it was I who shattered my own heart. When we next spoke, she indicated that had I returned the following day, everything could have been salvaged; instead, she had adjusted to the absence and sought merely to retain a friendship. Our paths did not intersect again until the school year resumed. As fate would have it, it would take nearly five years before I would again know the intimate affection of a girlfriend.

The beginning of the school year felt different. There was no excitement in the air, just a kind of dullness that seeped into me willingly. Another girl asked if I would accompany her to the ball. It seemed the word had spread, and I was the fool they sought. I tried to care; I attended a few practices, but my thoughts were tangled. I lacked the means for a tuxedo. Instead, I thought of donning a simple suit. Then, when the time came to leave, I found myself without bus fare. Too foolish to make a call, I left her waiting. But fate intervened, and my friend Ken Mosby appeared to take my place, picking up the pieces of my negligence.

I went through the motions during the season but still defeated Glenville for the third year in a row. I was a true Tarblooder killer. I also received the badge of good fortune and was named the team's MVP. Following in Calvin's footsteps. Coach Brady approached me shortly after for a heart-to-heart talk. He was very sincere and wanted me to know that I could play football in college. He checked my grades, and they were slipping. He assured me that if I would just perform the way he knew I could, this would happen. That was great news to me as no player since I had been at Lincoln-West was in school playing football. Bubba was recruited by Coach Tressel of Baldwin Wallace College but only stayed half the year and then joined the Cleveland Fire Department. Calvin Williams and Eric Ball also went to Baldwin Wallace but also left for civil service jobs as Police Officers for the City of Cleveland. But all of that was not what I saw for my future. Over the next couple of months, we narrowed things down to three schools: Mt. Union, Findlay College and Ashland College. We were going to make College a reality, not just a dream. The volume of folks that were going through this same thing was huge and created a whole new culture that shaped the country politically and financially. The thing the "D.E.A.D"s was afraid of was happening. However, some of the seeds they planted were not ready for harvest.

Springtime was approaching, and my pager went off. I was shocked and quickly went to a pay phone, "Hey, you hit me up." then I heard the most wonderful thing, "Yes." Now, this was the first time Nellie had called me in 10 months. She asked if I was busy, and if not, how about stopping by. Do you think I hesitated? I wasn't even going to play it cool, so I quickly said, " I will be right over." I was missing everyone and was hoping they were all there. To my surprise, it was just her and John John.

We watched some TV, played some new Atari games, and then just talked and caught up on things. Before I knew it, it had gotten late and old habits began to rear their heads. The next thing I knew, we were in bed. There was no coercion, just mutually enjoying each other. Afterward, she said, "Let's just be friends." I was puzzled and asked, "Then what was this?" She then asked, "Can't we do this and still be friends." That just broke my heart. Looking back on it, she was totally correct in not being as serious as my feelings had me. But I was not into just hitting ass, so I just got up and left. I again found myself walking 99 blocks to the train station at Tower City. The whole time, I was thinking this felt strange. Even the way we did, it felt strange. I mean, I had never felt it before, and since then, I have felt it only seven more times in my life. Spring break is over, and I got another page from her. I quickly called and, before she could say anything, told her I'm on my way. Then she said, "No, I just wanted to tell you I am pregnant." Damn, Damn, Damn, they got me. I quickly replied, "Are you sure?" She then asked me to come over the next day. We talked about it and still concluded that we would be friends.

My ego couldn't handle it. That's the truth. So, in a

moment of pure foolishness, I asked if I was the father. I didn't think about her—about what she was feeling. All I could think about was how much simpler it would be. And then she exploded—just like that, the conversation fizzled out for a week. I spent that week sick with worry for her. Then my pager buzzed. It was her. She wanted to talk. Our situation felt like a trap like we were caught in a game where the odds were against us. I guess not every seed you plant takes root, but if you don't try, you're guaranteed to get nothing. Nellie had done her homework, and it turned out it would take more than three hundred dollars for the abortion she had chosen. That was her path, but we faced a problem. How could we get the money? She didn't want her family to know, and I certainly didn't want my mom to find out. So, that left one option: my Pops.

I was able to track him down, and we met at his apartment in Warrensville. I was as candid as I could be about the situation. Then Pops gave me a lesson that I would have had years earlier. He started by reminding me that as the male, I am supposed to be protecting the woman. Son, "You can't protect her if you don't protect yourself." I then told him about her being on the pill. He went on to say that my focus was on the wrong thing. She wasn't trying to hurt me; she was just the tool to harm me, and I was the tool that harmed her. He then asked, "Do you know who was using you as a tool?" I said, "No." He said, "Always remember that you can find out who is doing something to you by the results." The one who would want to hurt you is the one who is using the tool." "This whole thing is about destroying "North American" lives." "If you and this young lady get rid of the baby, for sure, you have taken away a "North American" life." "If you and her keep the baby and you guys are not together, what are the chances of success?" "I guarantee you some office has told her she can do this without her parents knowing, and those offices are in the colored folks' neighborhood through and through." "It's all done on purpose, and we have fallen for it." But you gotta keep your eyes peeled for these setups, feel me? The bait on this one was your desire for a family, chasing that change—it's real, it's heavy, and yeah, I shoulder the weight of that. That's when it hit me like a light flicked on. I can't stop folks from trying to do me dirt in these times, nah. I just gotta catch 'em in the act, protect my spirit so I can shield others, too. It's all about survival in this game, you know. I told him she wanted to do this thing in two days, but I wanted her to meet with him first. He was cool with it.

The next day, I reached out, hoping she'd ride with me after school to see Pops. But before the final bell rang, she disappeared like a whisper in the wind. I called her house, but silence answered back. Then, the next night, her mom picked up, her voice smooth and calm, like a warm summer breeze. She asked how I was and then dropped the bombshell that Nell had told them she was pregnant. My heart sank. "Okay, I'll come over," I replied, but she gently warned me against it —her dad was in a storm of emotions. The law in Ohio had already made choices for us; at this stage, there was no turning back. That night, I was determined, consequences be damned. I needed to find a way to support her, to lift her up. She wasn't there, but her stepmom, Annia, welcomed me. She sat me down, no blame on her lips, just a reminder that we needed to let things settle. They had taken Nell to New York for a procedure, and she'd be home soon. I felt grounded, like I had to face the music. They had made their choice, and in that moment, I felt the weight of a life lost. The D.E.A.D. had struck at my expense.

About a week later, I almost did it again. We were at Case Western Reserve for the City Track and Field Championships. That's us in the picture with the trophy. Right after taking a picture with our trophy, about fifty gang members with bats and sticks attacked anything that said Lincoln-West as we were leaving to board the bus.

The whole thing was going in slow motion as I watched them strike Dennis over and over before I could get to him. Then they began to beat on our girls, and I watched Tonya Marshal just fall to the ground after being hit. They were trying to run away after the assault, and two were running in the direction of Miranda. I got there in just a nick of time and grabbed one of the sticks they had dropped, trying to hop the stadium fence. Before I knew it, I struck this kid full throttle in the face, and everyone watched his face blow up like a balloon with the sound of a shoe crushing a roach.

I found myself on the ground, a swirl of frustration and regret swirling inside me. Coach Claude Holland from John Adams High, our rival in this strange game of life, somehow had everyone scattering like leaves in the wind. They said he flashed a gun, though I couldn't be sure. Years rolled by, and we discovered a connection, coaching against each other like old friends turned foes. What sticks with me the most are his words—they had a way of yanking me back to reality, like a melody breaking through the noise. I have held onto that technique, my lighthouse in storms, ever since. Dennis and Tonya caught their breath in the hospital for a couple of days; they made it through. But the scars I carry linger like a shadow —echoes of a trial concluded, but life forever changed, like a lab rat in a maze called desegregation, stumbling through an experiment that nearly cost me my soul.

A MAN NOW

On this day, June 5, 1983, I stand at the precipice of adulthood, having just graduated from high school at the tender age of 18. In this grand moment, I find myself not only as a scholar embarking on a new journey but also as a creator of life, embracing the mantle of financial responsibility. I carry within me a profound solitude, where the weight of my emotional landscape lies solely upon my own shoulders. Who am I in this monumental endeavor? I am, indeed, alone.

As I reflect upon these feelings, I understand that solitude is not a stranger but a companion that has walked beside me for some time. It is within this contemplation that I recognize the plight of those who were bused from Glenville to the west side—a symbolic act that transcends mere geography. To some, it might seem as though they were transitioning from one impoverished neighborhood to another, yet this perspective overlooks the profound implications of educational inequity that have scarred our past. It is imperative to acknowledge that these young souls, caught in the currents of systemic discrimination, may be unaware of the historical weight they bear. They are innocent observers, not comprehending the depths of injustice that have shaped their realities.

As the school year unfolds, I sense an aching separation from the collective identity that once defined me with my "Our Gangs". It is my hope that in time, as we strive toward justice and equality, they too will come to embrace the profound benefits of this shared educational experience—one that can uplift, empower, and unite us all. But now, for me, the stage is very different. I am a man who has been teed up for a golf slice shot directly into the woods. I need help if I am to go straight down the fairway. I just need a clue.

Both of my gangs were now thrust into adulthood in the mid-80s. While being inspired by the jello pudding man himself "Bill Cosby". Maranda and Doug in the military, Sheryl and Robin were at The Ohio State University, Dennis was running track at Michigan State, Tim was running track at the University of Akron, Nellie was at Kent State University, and the other three Calvin, Eric, and Bubba were still serving the City of Cleveland. My Trotwood group was pretty much the same, Daryl was in the military, Mike was at Wittenberg College, Kim was at the University of Cincinnati, Mo was at the junior college, then to the University of Kentucky, Dwight was at a junior college, then to University of Iowa and Keith was at The Ohio State University. We were miles away from each other but there would finally be something that could genuinely unify our development. Each and every one of us was carrying a virus. The virus of fear of failure from a newfound claim that anything in this world we wanted was possible so we have no excuse not to succeed on any level.

in my earlier years, I found myself devoid of a guiding male presence—one that might embody responsibility, reason, and sensibility. Time, that relentless forward force, beckons a reckoning. To equip myself for the unknown that lies ahead, I have resolved to forge an alliance dedicated to self-education, embodying the knowledge of aspirations—both internal and external. Thus, I assembled what I like to call my dream team.

The desegregation movement, much like a revealing light, laid bare the veils of ignorance that hindered comprehension. The crescendo of human expression and mutual acceptance reached staggering heights, compelling the media to reflect a society that was indeed closer to the truth of our shared existence. Hence, why not place trust in this newfound reality? It is from this movement that my dream team emerged.

The struggle for civil rights unfolds in two distinct acts. The inaugural act assails children, utilizing adults as unwitting agents of influence. The concluding act engages the adult molded by this first onslaught. The consequences of such crafted adults lead me to believe that those who participated in the desegregation efforts emerged fortified, unlike any previously existing minority groups. The measure of this success, stark and undeniable, is evident in the condition of "North Americans" in our present day.

It's time to hit the real world. After I submitted to the act of being a father I nearly stopped all recruiting visits and was preparing to get a job and take care of my kid. Now that this was no longer the case, I was down to two schools, Ashland College and Findlay College. I had been accepted to both. I just needed to make a decision, So I flipped a coin. Heads for Ashland and tails for Findlay. The winner was Findlay College, which was a private school just off I-75. I worked out all summer, just waiting for the first day of practice. It was exciting. I was actually the first of my grandmother's grandchildren to go to college and this made my mother proud. I was still just thinking about football, though. I have yet to think about anything that would be related to a career, major or degree. The only thing in my life that I liked up to that point was football and no one had even talked to me about how this adult thing works. So what are my chances at this college thing?

Now, I was not the only one in this situation. The Brothers and sisters were now going to college by the boatload. We learned through our high school years and Bill Cosby that this is what we are supposed to do. The why was still blurry for most. For years now, we had attended schools with all types of kids, so going to white colleges and universities was no longer an intimidating factor. It was actually a cool preferred thing and there were plenty of colleges to go around. This wave of "North Americans" into academia was in volumes unlike anything in this country's past, and man, did we shape the world. The colleges loved this because it meant money, money, money.

The country was in a state of high inflation and low employment, so this set the colleges apart from those lows. The primary source of funds to go to college came from loans, grants and scholarships. This became a hustle and the unemployment disposition of the country allowed us to qualify for more aid because of the financial dispositions of our divided families. Yet, we found ourselves compelled to comprehend the intricate workings of this peculiar enterprise. As the initial generation from our families to tread the halls of academia, we possessed neither the guidance of tradition nor the mentors of experience to steer our course through this complex vessel. The answer, somewhat paradoxically, emerged from a source we would not have anticipated: the media. Television assumed the role of our primary educator, imparting lessons on how to converse, attire ourselves, amuse, aspire, unite, engage in leisure, celebrate, and even love. This cultural transmission extended to both black and white students alike, and we embraced it all as we plunged into college.

Man, it was my first day in that Findlay College cafeteria, and lo and behold, who do I see strutting in like she owns the place? This tall, slim, fine thing—had me thinking of a million-dollar bill, you know what I mean? I'm talking about Liana Lowery, but to me, she was "Flashdance." Looked just like that Jennifer Beals, that star in the movie where everybody was sweatin' and shakin' it, just dancing like nobody's business. Now, see, I figured out early in life that folks love to compare themselves to what's on the screen. You call someone by the name of a beautiful person and bam! They know you think they're a looker, and everyone else around hears it, too. So I started calling her "Flashdance" everywhere I saw her. In the gym, I'd be like, "Hey, Flashdance, what's up?" In the library, I was still "How you doing, Flashdance?" Game room? Same story, "Yo, Flashdance, how's it hanging?" Before you know it, she didn't stand a chance; I had that girl wrapped around my finger! You just gotta put it out there. This surprised some upper-class men, but hey, they didn't have my game. The dangerous part of this was more directed from the "D.E.A.D"s. This game was not just something I was using but it was at the core of cultural changes across the nation. I used the media as my game, and television now gave people a window to see that a lot of the stereotypes folks had been teaching for years were wrong.

The year is 1983 my girl "flash dance" escorts me up to her room. I have been waiting for some one-on-one time to see if we had a physical chemistry. Up to this point, it was all social. We get to her room and who is there? Her roommate, a cool white girl who was dating a black cat from the team, Cooper was his name. Now, I didn't worry because Coop could take his girl to her room, and I could get that chance to feel my "flash dance" out. Then, this box gets in the way. They turn on the TV, and another friend "Foots" comes in, "It's time for General Hospital". Now, I am like, did I just join a girls club. So, I am buying my time, just laying in the same bed, but no touchy things going on. It was odd as she was not very well endowed on the upper half. Yeah, she had little tits. So, I actually really wanted to see what they looked like wondering how I could fondle her top side. Then I got bamboozled. The show was actually great. I was in a room with these emotionally charged chics and this emotional love story of Luke and Laura was going on. It was like Larry and Leanna in my head. I was so addicted that I couldn't go to class and wasn't thinking about hitting it. I found myself looking at the new wave of black roles on television as a replacement for what I did not get from being raised in a divided home. My first-round draft pick was Luther Vandross, followed by Denzel Washington. I had an interpersonal recruiting forum for media stars to arm me for this war as an adult. Believe it or not, this is where I learned about the different occupations a black man could have. These became my mark. But not without some failures.

This new media wave of the 80s let people be together and for the most part, they have chosen to integrate. This caught the "D.E.A.D" 's social critics off guard as we made what was on TV a reality, starting with the parties.

"The roof, the roof, the roof is on fire. We don't need no water. Let the mother fucker burn. Burn mother fucker burn" Man, I felt bad about "flash dance" but we needed a car for the weekend and these white chicks had em. My boy L.C., from Warren, Ohio, had a redhead, and I had a brunette. Now, L.C. would freak his groupies to get the car. Me, I still had "Flashdance" so I would just lie. Bowling Green State University, University of Toledo, and Lima, Ohio were the spots. We were so dumb. We had these white chick cars running up and down I-75 and had no license at all or gas money. The car would be loaded, though, with my roommates from Cincinnati, Drew and Butch as well.

After you go to the same parties a couple of times, you get to know cats, and cats get to know you. While at a party in

Toledo, who do I ran into, Donald Williams (Don Juan). Don was the infamous leader of the D.D. gang back when I was in high school. He didn't recognize me at first and I felt so stupid afterward because I thought I was at a party for college cats only. These parties had turned into atmospheres for anyone that wanted to do his hustle. My dumb butt asked Don, "What school you go to? I really didn't care because we had a history, and I thought that meant a little something. He just gave me a look and sipped his drink.

Now, most of those parties ended with a fight. This one was no different. Neither he nor I started it. But we were next to each other, making sure these fraternity cats didn't get a lick in. After everyone started running from the police, I was able to reminisce with him about those crazy fights at Lincoln-West with the racists in the neighborhood. Then the light went on for him and he remembered. "Man, what yo punk ass doing out here?" I looked at him, "I am just here with my boys from Cincinnati and Toledo for the party. We go to Findlay College down the road." He went, "Shit, dude, I thought you were in the game, then he pulled out a wad of dough. "We are making a killing out here with this California shit." Man, I don't like riding out here all the time though, how often you and the Cincinnati boys go home." I go, "Why?" He told me, "Man, I'm waiting for my boys from Cinci and you know where home is. Yawl, can get some of this money and save me a drive."

Now, I am about to be shot. "D.E.A.D" is trying to hit me where it hurts, my freedom. Here was this easy money right in front of me. I imagined that I was Eddie Murphy in "Trading Places", he was down and out, they gave him dough, but in the end, it was a trap. My reply was, "I'm good," and I walked away. That was not the last time we crossed paths but I was blessed by Eddie Murphy that night.

This became my pattern. The media during that time

fueled us as a virus and had hidden positive messages that our generation could model after. Many of the songs and storylines would fill in the gaps that many had because of being raised by one parent. We had something positive to model after, unlike shows like "Good Times" of the 70s. It became a gold mine as the world just followed us as we were growing, and the money was too good for the media not to have these positive portrayals for the first time.

My list started with the Gumby Dammit" Eddie Murphy. I fell in love with the beauty, elegance and strength of the roles of Diana Carol, a black woman who was lusted by black and white men on TV. The athlete wasn't the character of strength, it was "Tubbs" from 'Miami Vice". Rating showed how many were watching. While an all-white show like Mash with an all-white doctors cast came to an end. Now we had a black doctor in Denzel Washington. Oh, and there was this superhero called "Panty Man" yeah, this cat Spike Lee aka MARS whore panties on his head. Not just blacks but the whole world could see we were no different and great.

Then, I get a road map to success. The pudding pops dad himself. The Bill Cosby Show became my model, similar to Mr. Willis for my pops. Except Bill had the full orchestra. Man, they taught me how to dress, walk, talk, accept the finer things life had to offer and pride. The biggest hole of mine that was filled was how to be a parent. Parenting was the thing for us that "D.E.A.D" was trying to dismantle, and for me, it was put back together in one swift move with The Cosby Show. Then there were movies. people could now identify with each other. Diana Carroll slaps an "American"(white) woman on national TV. Denzel is introduced to us as a "North American" Doctor in Miami Vice. a brother and "American" dude are fighting crime together. We could have money and jobs and the media showed us the way in more ways than you thought. We were getting stable and destabilization was their next move.

Meanwhile, back home in Cleveland, the "D.E.A.D" thought had put a dagger in our hearts as they ended desegregation. What they didn't realize was the damage was done and the short period of time of desegregation solidified us as a unique generation of children. The only and last of its kind. This move aggressively attacks the next generation. If they were weak, death was almost a sure thing. Grandparents raising babies was at an all-time high in the late mid to late 80s due to crack cocaine in the hands of post-desegregation kids and the HIV epidemic for post-desegregation kids.

My sister Bonita gets married to this dude, Tony Bryant. They move in with his parents. Mamma is now dating one of my uncle's buddies, friends from West Virginia, Joel Medley and the family now moves into his home in Cleveland Hts. Guess who now lives two blocks over from the Medleys? The Dobbins family. Nells, dad had a stroke and everyone was trying to adjust. They had always owned the home in Cleveland Heights. but had been renting it out. For me this was more about supporting them than it was trying to get with her. I felt I owed them for some reason.

All of this new mental stimulus had me on cloud nine. Then I saw for the first time live and in person someone that I knew take an act of true freedom through understanding who he was and what he meant to the world. It still resonates with me today. Gerald Dowe, man, he was the linebacker you didn't mess with, like a grizzly bear that just woke up from hibernation and is hungry. Picture this: it's early morning, the sun just teasing the horizon, and I'm strolling back to my dorm like a lost puppy when I spot Gerald out by his car, wrestling with his laundry like he's got weights in his hands. Now, I don't know why, but the dude's got the soul of a philosopher today, right? He looks at me, all serious, and says, "Fool, I gotta stop playing myself." I'm thinking, "What's this about?" Then he drops this bomb: "All these girls, they're just taking up space, man! I'm not getting anything from them, or these classes for that matter. I just go in, grab a grade faster than a cheetah on roller skates so I can get back on that field for Coach Strahm, you feel me?" And he's like, "They're using me, putting me up on some fake pedestal. I gotta get my life together, start treating myself right, do something real." It was like he was looking in the mirror and finally seeing the dude staring back, ready to trade in the party for something that actually matters." That was the last time I saw Gerald. I heard he was a pastor in Jacksonville, Florida now. I thought he had everything, at the games, the students would make posters of him to hand around the stadium, and the coaches did whatever he asked. He had a superhero title like Batman and Robin. It was 747. Charles Dukes, a killer end, was 7, and Gerald Dowe, the Killer linebacker, was 47.

Man, how could he just stroll off like nothing? I mean, this hit me like a ton of bricks, and suddenly, I'm looking in the mirror, asking myself, "What the hell am I doing?" And the truth? I'm just wandering around like a lost dog without a bone. I hadn't set foot in half my classes since they dragged me in on the first week. No major—just this wild notion that if you play college ball, the pros are lining up to hand you a check. Hold on a second! I'm at a Division 2 NAIA school— ain't even close to the big leagues that are on ESPN, and look, NCAA Division 1 is the only game in town on TV. Not to mention there's like 30-something NFL teams and a hundred college squads—all fighting for a tiny spot in the league. Damn, I'm on the wrong path! I finally see what's going on, Gerald.

"NORTH AMERICAN" MAN

It's Thanksgiving break. My head is getting clearer by the day. Funny thing is, the more my head began to clear, the more independent and responsible I began to feel. I just needed more info to formulate a plan. I get home, and man, God is funny. My state of mind, married with what I run into, was clearly an example of how steps are ordered, and he prepares me for the next step. It's just that sometimes the pain is so bad I get blinded and weak in the knees that I can't see or even walk down the path he has drawn for me.

I've got a bullet lodged in my heart, courtesy of the nights spent alone. You could call it loneliness, my friend. A cat like me knows that life's twists and turns come whether you're ready or not, whether someone loves you or you pour your love into a void. The suffering's a kind of pain that's so profound you'd trade just about anything to shake it off—even your own existence. But I carry on, a bit of a fighter, and that's perhaps the only reason I'm still standing, battling the aching silence that loneliness has hurled at me.

As I scribble this tale, I see that what folks might call love—a sweet connection—is little more than aspirin for my heartache. I've come to grips with the fact that my own choices set the stage for this whirlwind of life changes since I made that fateful cut and sent Pops down his own road away from ma. The names of people have become like different brands of pain relief, each holding a little magic and a lot of heartache—be it "Bayer Aspirin" or "Excedrin" or something heavier like "codeine." It all blends into a mosaic of souls: friends, colleagues, family, lovers—each part of the same fabric weaving a tapestry of relief, yet somehow, they all remind me of the pain beneath. It's a peculiar thing, this human connection, a dance of joy mixed with the bittersweet reality of life.

Webster's dictionary defines lonely as: without anyone or anything else; not involving or including anyone or anything else; separate from other people or things; without people that you know or that usually are with you. The pain is that kind of aching that resonates in your chest. That dull, constant feeling that follows you around all day. I do believe loneliness is marked by a sense of isolation.

The firing pins are rejections. I need help. This loneliness is the weapon I will be fighting for the rest of my life with hopes and prayers that I can withstand the pain and not let it re-shape the man I am meant to be.

While waiting on a ride to Cleveland, the only thing on TV was the news. The crazy politics of that day would actually save my life. Our dear President Ronald Reagan set into motion two life-altering epidemics with his decision-making towards HIV and the Nicaraguan war. I keep watching this dude Oliver North on TV, and he just flat-out tells lies with the actor Reagan backing him up. Reagan got this thing down. After all, he was an expert at putting actions into motion that took lives as he was the outspoken California leader my dad talked about who made sure of the all-out assault on the Black Panthers. The things folks were doing to survive were taking us back to the medieval days. I have bigger problems, though.

A modern-day slave trade was put into play. Whole communities needed funds. The bondsman and overseers of the old slave institution fed their families for years based on the management of slaves. The D.E.A.D. needed them alive as a commodity. Through the mix of things learned during prohibition and the drug crisis after Vietnam, a perfect storm was created with the government's assistance in flooding the inner cities with crack cocaine. Oliver North's Iran contra affair. is aired on TV finally, even though we have been talking about it for years in the club.

The primary source for cocaine to enter the country is our government. I am in college now and it is finally substantiated. The hood isn't capable of cooking the powder to a crystal form called crack without help. Bolivians had the powered cocaine and needed financial support for their war. In 1988, this was admitted on national television as the Medellin cartel was under interrogation by then-Senator John Kerry. The brothers in the inner city would get their small change cut. Our government now had a divided intercity in every metropolis across the nation.

In throwing the rock and hiding the hand, President Reagan had to help and Crack Laws were put into play, sending billions of federal dollars into the fight. Reagan signs the bill and a candy bar size will get you 10 to life and employment longevity for those who housed you in their prisons. The war on drugs was on. Filling our stables with slaves again was the call vs. just not letting cocaine in. It's kind of ironic how a white material of trade is always at the center of slavery. 300 years earlier, it was cotton, now cocaine.

Man this was slick because there go the voters, Dr. King gave his life for. This is the start of the fall of inner cities, especially when married with the constant attack of

"D.E.A.D," and we get modern-day East Cleveland, East St Louis, etc.

Pace of action becomes key to identifying when shots fired by "D.E.A.D"s are heading directly at you. During this time of Reaganomics, folks were selling blood just to survive. The country becomes aware that heterosexuals now carry the HIV virus. Governmental funds are now being given for a cure after this white kid Ryan caught aid, and his community forced his parents to pull the kids from his school just like they did before we were bused to Lincoln-West.

But it saved my life because of this public health crisis. Trojans. No condoms, no sex. The fight was now with angry white males against "D.E.A.D"s. They even hung a white man in public. Yes, that's what I said. and it was President Ronald Reagan. ACT UP was their name. They held them off for enough time that I was able to slide in and have not looked back. Years earlier, through experiments of their own for medicine, some sources... taught those leftover some new trick... The Ryan White Act... nine hundred million dollars. for the federal disaster. The world was calling it an American problem, with one million cases there alone vs 5 million for the rest of the world.

In the meantime, Reagan had to help with federal court cases. Lynn Bias' death from cocaine on the public scene was the catalyst. Congress now can adopt Crack Laws. Reagan signs the bill..a candy bar size will get you 10 to life...In any state. Now, they officially use the word war. The war on drugs.

When I got home for Thanksgiving, I found my brother just sitting on the steps. Now, this was odd but I had not seen him since the summer, so it was cool. Now, this fool sits with me and we catch up for about 45 min. Then I asked him, "Where is mom?" He goes on to tell me that she went to West Virginia. I was like," Let's get out the cold." Then he took me for a loop. UUhhh, "They won't give me a key to the house, so

I have been on the streets. Having a clear understanding about what was in those streets, I equated that to putting him to death.

"Now, for me, blood is thicker than water. "How long they have been gone." "About three days, but they should be back tonight or tomorrow." Now, I am not about to sleep outside and had become a master at breaking into our home as a teenager who was always out late. I go to the side of the garage, get the ladder and place it on the second-floor window. As usual, it was not locked,; and we were in. Tony went on to tell me how he and my mom's husband weren't getting along and that he didn't give my mother a choice but to put her son on the streets. Now, I am starting to go into beast mode. Then I hear the door opening. Now, we were still upstairs when they got home. Before they could say anything, I called out, "Is that you, ma."

Joel Medley proceeded, let's just say it got ugly, and we spent that Holiday at 1773 Hower. Going back, there was no longer an option. The United States Military now has me but in reserve status, till school starts.

HIDING IN ASHLAND

After breaking down some of my experiences during boot camp to my mother, Joel Medley attempted to mend the fences by educating me on the Government bombing of our own people in Philly, The Family Africa. He went on to explain this was going on while I was in camp, and white folks were finally happy someone had the balls to do something to niggers(black). For the most part, this gave him a chance to just talk to someone and get ideas and thoughts out of his head and into an intelligent mind. This gave us an understanding that would last till he passed and saved me from killing him one last time. I was still on edge, though.

While going through basic training, I experience one of the most horrific events of my life. I mean, it was to the point that I was like, let me die. My mind could not comprehend the purpose behind why they would do this to people. Their reasoning was that it could save my life one day. For me, it was more like taking my life right now. I guess people are built differently. Oh, so much snot. I mean, snot on everyone from head to toe. Man, the jokers made us put on a gas mask and walk into a building. Then they closed the door and filled the room with gas, told us to take off the mask and made us just stand there even after we could no longer hold our breath. The pain, oh, the pain. Every ounce of mucus that your body had in it found its way out. You just wanted it to go away. It did not teach me the value of keeping the mask on. It taught me that if I get gas, just shoot myself in the head.

When I got to boot camp, I was in top shape. I planned to stay that way as I was transferring to Ashland University to do this thing the right way. Gerald Dowe's way. It was cool. I maxed out my first P.T. test and Ashland was constantly sending me mail. I had no military Jane so we corresponded back and forth a lot. The way they treated me was now different. I didn't get yelled at, I was given extra food and time off. I was like they know who the man is. During the last week you take the last P.T. exam. My God, I could not run, did maybe 40 push-ups and my sit-ups were non-existent. If they did not average both scores together I would not have even graduated. Then the truth showed its face. At graduation, they gave away awards, and one was for the top P.T. score. I missed it by one point. I was just sabotaged by my own people and had football camp shortly.

Ashland College, as it was called back then, was one of the

republican strongholds of the State. There were some really kind folks with good intentions grounded on making it to heaven, but at every turn, "D.E.A.D"s. was there and it didn't take long before I had to deal with it head-on. My new group of boys was Daryl Robertson, Reggie Simms, Chris Harkness, The Rev Mark Cunningham and Jimmy Mitchel. We were the 'North American' freshmen and members of the football team that's us on the top row, me, Daryl, Coach Martinelli and Coach Jefferson or lone "North American". and next to him was my running back coach, who committed suicide after the season because his wife divorced him.

I was the oldest, had a car and lived off campus as it was the only way I could afford to go to school. Now, Daryl, Reggie, Chris and I had been on campus for about three weeks with the football team before the official start date of school. When the rest arrived, it was party time. The first weekend here, we were in a white frat house and even though some were our teammates, you could tell they didn't want us there. I knew to just have some free beer and chill while checking out the scene.

All of a sudden I see one of the boys with an old school car jack. The kind that clicks into old 1970s cars with metal bumpers. He liked the white girls, but the frat boys weren't having it. The "D.E.A.D" 's children showed their faces and if you were white at that moment, you were wrong as far as he was concerned. No one got hurt as I facilitated peace. What came next set the tone for the rest of my life. I believed I had the attention of Coach Fred Martinelli, a man whose presence loomed large in the halls of sport. So, I took the liberty of dialing his number, hoping to bring him into the fold of our pressing situation—a bid to steady the tempers of my rural teammates, who, with their shotguns securely stashed in their pick-up trucks, were not a calming presence. The line was filled with a profound stillness, his response but a whisper, a simple thank you, before the connection severed. There was an inherent goodness in his heart, a fundamental decency that rendered him incapable of inflicting harm upon us. His silence, however, was not an absence but a means of cultivating tranquility.

In an adjacent realm, our library stood replete with tomes of wisdom; only yesterday, I had unearthed Kenneth Stamp's compelling work, The Peculiar Institution. Within its pages were written the five steps by which the so-called "North Americans" might be made to cower in trepidation, an unsettling reflection of our own fraught circumstances.

1. Establish and maintain strict discipline.
2. Implant in the slave consciousness of personal inferiority.
3. Awe, the bondsman with a sense of the master's power.
4. Persuade the slave to take an interest in the master's enterprise and to accept his standards of good conduct.
5. Impress in the slave his utter sense of helplessness to create a habit of perfect dependence.

In a covert fashion, the silence by Coach put into play the five steps, with the white players who were on the attack being the bondsmen. Today, we just call them the privileged.

My focus quickly turned to getting out as soon as I could, but not without the degree. I did have a conversation with my running back coach about it. My awareness of the world around us all was greater than the game and thus, I was no longer an athlete who could be blindly coached. I clearly understood Gerald Dowe's statement. My remaining time at Ashland became a blur as I ducked and dogged "D.E.A.D"s attacks over and over as they tried to implement the five guidelines to creating a good Nigger. Reading became my outlet. This also steered me to the Sociology and Criminal Justice classes. The political environment of the day was centered on Reaganomics. There is money in crime so my major will now be "Criminal Justice and Sociology". This is how I got a badge on my heart and gun on my waist.

There were some catalytic events that aided in my focus. I had found love for the second time in Robin Griggs. She was this girl that slept on the couch underneath me on the night of the fake orgy party at Miranda's on the night of the football championship game. Her looks reminded me of Spike Lee Nola Darling and that scared me. While I was going through boot camp, we wrote back and forth and she was down to earth. Of course, my ego fucked it up. I had never gotten my driver's license and had been driving for a couple of years. I was taking her and her cousin back to school at Ohio State when I got pulled over for speeding. Now, you know they locked me up. Robin got $300.00 and bailed me out of jail. It was a quick process with the court; just came back with a driver's license, and all I would have is a fine. My embarrassment was so deep I never went to see her again. Yep, I was a punk. It was like one disaster after another, leading to loneliness. Over that Christmas break, my running back coach commits suicide. The "D.E.A.D"s had loaded their guns again. He was the one coach I was willing to give 100%. Now, I had no girl, no coach, no family. The "D.E.A.D"s had loaded their guns again. Once again, I was alone.

THE WORLD IS A CRAZY BLENDER

Webster's dictionary defines lonely as: without anyone or anything else; not involving or including anyone or anything else; separate from other people or things; without people that you know or that usually are with you. For me, it created a pain the kind that causes an aching that resonates in your chest. That dull, constant feeling that follows you around all day. I do believe loneliness is marked by a sense of isolation. If one could harness loneliness, it could be as dangerous as a nuclear bomb. If someone would drop that bomb the desired outcomes are almost guaranteed to be full devastation. I am beginning to think this is the "D.E.A.D" 's number one weapon for me.

In the winter break of 1987, all the students had gone home and I had been sleeping with an odd chill all day. You ever tried to wake up from a dream and found yourself frozen stiff? I was paralyzed and could not move a limb. Somehow, I was able to reach my phone. I hit redial my accident instead of 911. I then heard the loveliest squeaky voice. I had called a dear friend, Lisa. I explained my symptoms and she said, "I am on my way". It felt like seconds had passed by and I could hear her knocking at the door. It's 3:00 am and Lisa was here looking out for me. Not to my surprise, she was with her boyfriend, a Sheriff from Richland County. Damn, she got out of the bed with her man to check on me. She was indeed a friend for life. I had pneumonia and she was able to get the lonely dude through the night till he could see a doctor. Today, I claim us as angels for each other as she more than likely saved my life; but I now feared being alone.

I had never been in an interracial relationship, although many opportunities had come my way. I guess I was caught up in the fear that, ultimately, the fear of her upbringing would become my demise. My two best friends during the desegregation experiment Eric and Dennis, were both stood up by their white prom dates. But after almost dying the scale of fear tipped to the side of the companion and here came Amy. She was a cool chick from Rochester, New York, who had been eying me all school year. If this means not being alone, let's take the chance. Stupid, Stupid, Stupid me. The "D.E.A.D." shot me five times with this one. It's amazing I am here.

This was the pre-cellphone era and long-distance phone calls were at a premium. She would walk the campus with me as I was performing my paid duties. I would be in and out of offices and sometimes I would notice her on the phone. I didn't pay it any mind as they could be used to call into your dorm. We had another break and she went home a couple of days after the rest of the students so that we could chill, and I fought off that fear of being alone. I then drove her home to Rochester but was not allowed to meet her folks. When everyone was asleep, she called my beeper and gave me a number to call. She then snuck me in the back door leading to the basement where her bedroom was located. Man, I was so scared of being in these "American"(white) folks' houses in the middle of the night and no one knew where I was. It was so bad that I couldn't even get Mr. Happy up. It didn't matter what she tried, he wasn't having it. Needless to say, without getting any sleep, I got out of that house and rolled down the road.

I was clearly in the "D.E.A.D"'s sites. Man, let me tell you, I woke up from this crazy dream, right? All I could think about was the cops rolling up on me, my bare backside exposed, while I'm just, ya know, trying to do my thing with this "American" girl, and all I hear is her yelling, "rape, rape!" Now that's a nightmare! My brain was stuck on repeat, like a bad record. Then, outta nowhere, bam! I'm jolted awake by this loud BOOM. Turns out I'd been cruising through dreamland like I'm in NASCAR, but now I'm bumpin' against the guard rail at 3 AM. Now I'm sittin' there like, "What in the world am I doing?" Here I am, somewhere in Pennsylvania, flat out catching Z's on the side of the road, alone like a lost sock in the dryer, and no one even knows where I am! Back then, no cell phones, so I had to sneak my way to the nearest exit to find a pay phone – you remember those? I'm burnin' through the last of my phone card minutes trying to reach Amy, but she ain't pickin' up! All I wanted was to tell her, "Hey, I'm still alive, just in case my luck runs out and I don't make it back to Ashland!" So, after a six-hour snooze that felt like six years, I finally limped my bent-up ride back home. Shot number one, ya know what I'm saying.

That afternoon I was called into the office of the Safety Services Director Don Maroney. He was a clean cut former trooper with a bad back just trying to get his daughter through college for free. He presented me with a phone bill of a list of long-distance calls made to Rochester New York. He further added that they had spoken to Amy on the other end of the calls, and she indicated that it was I who had made some 40-plus calls to her. The total was around $250.00. I was in the sights of "D.E.A.D"s. He needed $250.00 asap or I was catching a case.

Of course, I paid. Before paying, I asked to see the list and saw the number I had for her only twice. I dialed the number from the office, right? And who picks up? Amy! Man, she was all over the place, crying like she just found out her favorite show got canceled. She's like, "I had to do it or my parents would have killed me, and then I can't come back to school to be with you!" I'm sitting there thinking, what are you crying for? I'm the one in hot water here! Then she hits me with, "He hurt me, he hurt me!" And I'm like, oh man, here we go, who hurt you, your dad, 'cause I look like trouble. But then she throws me for a loop. "No, not him! This guy from high school!" What? I'm there like, when did this even happen? So she spills the tea: "After you left, I snuck out to see him. I felt all rejected and just wanted to chat it up. But things got wild, and we ended up having sex—though I didn't really want to!" I'm standing there, mouth open, like, girl, you better be kidding me. That was the straw that broke the camel's back and I was done. This chick just fucked me all around.

When school starts, I am really focused. This is it: I am going to be a college graduate. The first of my grandmother's and grandfather's grandchildren from both sides of the family, the first of my mom and pops. This was 1988 and it was hard to believe this would be the first. This was about more than me. It represents their struggle as well. Then you know who shows up. "D.E.A.D"s. This time, in the form of a Whitney Houston hairstyle, a beautiful cocoa girl getting out of brown Mercedes SEL. This was the big body one but hers was not bad either, and man, I could sit a glass on that ass. My Johnson was on full attention, and that had never happened before. I put my Denzel Washington face on. Sucked on the right side of my bottom lip and stepped to the entire family with my eyes glued on her the whole time. "Let me help you guys get unloaded. " Her pops gave me the look, her mom smiled with big eyes and she said "Sure" and gave me the smile of a lifetime.

The girl's name was Kim and I was in heaven. While getting her unloaded, I was introduced to Mr. Moore, her stepfather, who was a manager at the Ford plant in Cleveland and Mrs. Joyce Moore, her mother. It was crazy how the conversations between the four of us covered 18 years of her life. By the time we had unloaded, I knew she was originally from Detroit and Graduated from Benedictine High School, her father was in prison, and her grandparents were still in Detroit. They were now living in Elyria, Ohio so that Mr. Moore could get to work on the West Side of Cleveland and still get in and out of Detroit so that he could see his two sons and get his wife and stepdaughter to Detroit to see their loved ones. Man, it was like I just fit in. Before they pulled off, leaving her for her first night in college, I felt like their son.

After work, I spent the rest of the night with Kim. We talked and laughed, had something to eat, then talked some more and before we knew it, the sun was rising. I don't know what came over me but before I left to go home, I asked her to marry me. She unsurprisingly said yes. Man, what a relief my loneliness is over. That year, I was focused.

We won. I graduated from college, Ashland in 1989, and now I need to get out of dodge as fast as possible. I had won this battle but "D.E.A.D"'s was hard at work on the rest of the black community. Their fruits from crack cocaine and the HIV epidemic had Grandparents raising babies, the incarceration rate was at an all-time high, desegregation was gone, and the division was taking root again. Me and Kim set a wedding date on her birthday, June 16, 1990. We took a trip to Detroit so I could meet some of her old schoolmates. On the trip, I got the chance to visit my uncle Billy for the first time. He is the brother standing in the middle with all the melanin in his skin.

I was amazed at his wall of gold records from so many stars but what really stood out was his picture and story of him and Donnie Simpson and what they did for "North Americans" and the creation of BET. He gave back to the world. My little cousins and his children have followed in his footsteps. Lauren Speed Hamilton starred in the reality show "Love is Blind" and I  can't wait for their "North American" child. While Nick is laying beats down for the nation's best hip-hop artist. It was my turn to give back and East Cleveland is where it all began, so here I come. I took the apartment above my grandparents, just as the most successful man in the family had. I would have to be there without Kim, as she had one more year of college left. This separation is a gamble, with the price being loneliness.

GAME TIME

What we do transcends color, and we are the very force required by this land we call America—a land where we nurture its promise with the best we have to offer. In this great nation, there's little room for weakness, particularly the kind that limits our intellect. I am proud to declare that I am "100% American," "North American," from the very core of my being—from the structure of my cheeks to the rhythm of my steps. There's a uniqueness to America that simply cannot be replicated; no one moves or thinks quite like us. Much like parents of adopted children often guard the truth of their origins, we—within the fabric of this nation—also hold close the complex narrative of our minority brothers and sisters, those of us with rich melanin. I stand here, as a North American, not defined or diminished by my color but embodying the very essence of what it means to take our rightful place. Together, we are all part of this tapestry, a testament to the strength found within every corner of our great nation. We are the culmination of diverse humanity, each one of us contributing to the promise and power of America. The Etymology of the word "nigger" was derived from an

English word "neger," that was itself derived by "Word Back Formation," which is the creation of a new root word by the removal of a phantom affix in this case, "ro" from "Negro", the Spanish word for black. Their language was the dominant one at the onset of modernizing American when it was discovered. Thus, the when you call me "Black," you are also calling me "Nigger" The charge of those who were blessed with the integration created by desegregation is to live a life the same as any man or woman in this land as we are united forever as North Americans.

It's time to see how powerful and impactful we will be because of it. I must keep my head on swivel as there are still folks who had Devoted Efforts Against Desegregation the civil rights movement and its outcomes, the ones I call "The D.E.A.D." Hence, the opening paragraph. I am "North American". That equals being a trailblazer no different than that "American" named Elvis.

I began coaching football at my high school, Alma Mater Lincoln-West along with teaching at a middle school within the school district. This was the school district that "American"(white) folks fought so hard to keep segregated. I was quickly seen as an asset to several schools and found a home at the displaced Margaret Spellacy Middle School. There were some undiagnosed fumes that had students falling out, so they split the students into two different locations. The principal needed a young go-getter to help keep things together among students and staff. Deja Vu, this time, I am getting paid. By the spring, I was the head track coach. I used what my old hall of fame coach Bump Taylor gave to me, and to their surprise, we had success. That snowballed into referrals to other jobs, then "D.E.A.D"s. strikes.

By school's end, Kim had also graduated, and the wedding was scheduled for her birthday on June 16th. I had all my boys lined up: Eric, Dennis, Tim, Pup, Doug, etc. The girls were all in line up from Miranda, Cheryl, Alicia, etc. Two days before the wedding, the fellas gave me a customary bachelor party. It was like a house party of parties. Before I knew it, I was handcuffed, butt naked with some chick riding Mr. Pickle with fellas pouring beer all over us while she took turns tasting their pickles. The price I paid was tremendous, as the boys didn't think of putting a condom on Mr. Pickle. She rode it and rode it and rode it. The whole time I just keep thinking, what is this bitch giving me. While that was happening, some of the drunk fellas began to damage the house, and we all had to spit. The rest of the night was memorable as we found our way onto the fifty yard line of the Cleveland Browns Municipal Stadium with the lights on and simulated old high school football plays before more strip clubs. By the time I had cleared my head from that night, I had less than 24 hours before the wedding.

It was a beautiful ceremony in Elyria, Ohio. Then, as soon as the "I Dos" were done, I could see the wounds of the shots fired. As the girls began to congratulate Kim I sensed an uneasy feeling. Then, ironically Alicia somehow got red lipstick all over Kim's white wedding dress. Shortly after that, one of the fellas asked me how the hoe was they got me the other night. I replied was she a real hoe, like a prostitute. He replied, "hell yeah". I'm like, I gotta get me some condoms for tonight. I used a money problem with the DJ as an excuse and went looking for some condoms. A trip that should have taken 10 minutes lasted 45, and I still did not get any condoms. Man, I am tripping. Now, Mr. Pickle, brown Pickle that is, was feeling ok but not in the clear as it had only been a little over 24 hours since that whore rode him. How fucked up would it be to give my wife a STD on our wedding night. DAmn Damn DAMN!

Needless to say, when we got to the hotel, I played the real sleepy role and fell asleep without consummating the wedding. That morning, she was hot, like mad. She was so hot the only way I could try to calm her down was to give her Mr. Pickle anyway and just pray. Afterward, I realized the damage was done. A girl's dream is about the night of her wedding with her husband, not the morning. There was nothing I could do to correct it; we can't turn back the hands of time. She was heartbroken, and we weren't a day into marriage. It created an atmosphere of openness that led to her telling me she had been having second thoughts about getting married, but with all the planning, she just let it happen.

This hit me hard, ya know? Loneliness straight-up crashed into my soul. All I could think about was how I just stepped into this new life with someone who wasn't really there with me, and it felt like we lost a moment that was supposed to be ours forever. We might have the ring and the paper, but it was just for show. We even considered returning all those beautiful gifts and cash, untouched and pristine. I reached out to Pops, and somehow, he worked his magic, telling me we were just worn out from the wedding whirlwind and needed to let it breathe. I bet she got the same loving words from someone close. By the end of the day, we took a breath, changed our minds, and drifted off to sleep with Mr. Pickle slipping in and out of his jar, hoping for a sweeter dream.

For two young recent college grads we were living the TV dream. We lived above my grandparents, and through the track coaching gig, I was able to secure both of us a job at an organization called Phoenix Circle as managers of students for a summer work program. While waiting for school to start at the University of Akron, where Kim had been appointed Assistant Dean of Students. They were providing us with an apartment at Orr Hall as part of her compensation package. While I was in consideration for a couple of positions with the State of Ohio.

Time to grow up. Life was repeating itself as I began the new venture of helping the next generation. The young brothers needed help to arm themselves with skill sets that would help them when being confronted by the "D.E.A.D"s. They had no pawn moves. It was really needed as the attacks were crazy. I had been recommended to Buchtel H.S. in Akron, Ohio, as a football and track coach. Buchtel was by far the most renowned athletic school in the Akron area and had just come off of back-to-back State football titles led by Michigan running back Ricky Powers.

What a great place to learn! They had two Hall of Fame Coaches in, track coach William N. Heideman and football coach Tim Flossie. Their base was the core of knowledge that I would begin to steal. Now, my mentor was still my high school coach and State of Ohio Hall of Fame Coach Bump Taylor. Gaining knowledge from another State of Ohio Hall of Famer in Coach Heideman was just putting the icing on the cake. I was more interested in the management of the athletes' motivation and seasonal strategies than I was that of training.

Man, did I get some lessons from Buchtel while the "D.E.A.D"s was hitting the lottery?

In my first football season, I endured the first life loss of an athlete. He was a gritty, undersized nose-guard. One day, he was angry and went banging on the door of someone who was also angry at him over some drugs. Through this ignorant arrogance, he never thought of the next phase and was shot in the chest as the person on the other side of a door just decided to shoot through the door. What took me for a spin was the casual conversation about his death, as this was not an unusual occurrence. Not that it was acceptable, but it was not an unusual surprise. All I kept thinking about was how I could have saved this kid's life.

By the time track season had come around, circumstances had me listed as the Girls' Head Track Coach. I found it strange as his assistant John Scott was the truth. More than a Robin for Batman, this dude knew his stuff both on and off the track. Now, I was a bit arrogant as the young ladies I had previously coached while at Margeret Spellacy in Cleveland were now the core of the best team in the state at Collinwood High School. Heideman was really into the boy team as the girls' core were sophomores, so time for a chess move. I just did what I had in the past with family relationships at the core. Bump had instilled in us that our bond would be for life. It meant more than a coach and pupil being family. By season's end, I was voted co-coach of the year.

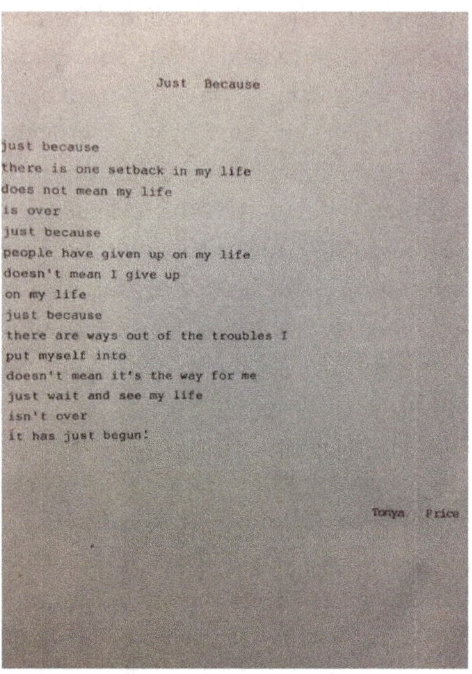

The "D.E.A.D"s appeared. Toward the end of the season, we learned that one of the young sprinters, Tonya Price, was pregnant. As a freshman, she placed 5th in the Finals in the 400m while at Medina H.S. The expectations were that she could win it now that she was at Buchtel. Tonya was having a rough time with how people were viewing her now that she was pregnant. She wrote me a poem called "Just Because" to express how she felt and how she was dealing with the humiliation of the situation. Over the summer, she went into labor. Unfortunately, Tonya gave her last breath, giving birth to a son.

After her death, I had a mentoring conversation with Coach Heideman. I used to pick at him for always popping aspirin before he would go on a run and did not realize till after that conversation that this dude had to be in his early 60s and was clearly pre-civil rights movement educated. It was a politically correct conversation that involved a chess move. He recommended to the county AD that I take over the boys at their rival high school, Central Hower, a promotion of sorts. I believe the girls were in good hands with the guru John Scott, so I transitioned smoothly and took over the boy's track program at Buchtel's rival high school, Central Hower. That was it for me, and I relentlessly went after a job with the State of Ohio. But, I continued my head coaching duties and mentoring as head boys Track and Field coach at Akron Central Hower High School. Because of it, I could relate to Lebron James and gang split/rivalry with the Griffs later in life. I had a great group of kids who over-achieved and had some success against the down-the-street boys as well, but only because we were family even till today. John Scott went on to become a State of Ohio Hall of Famer as well, which made me feel proud to have learned from such great minds.

Mr. Larry Ferguson
Head Coach Boys' Track

LIFE "I HEAR THE MUSIC"(CHESS NOT CHECKERS)

A brief history lesson on the foundation of my next move

"In 1866, one year after the 13 Amendment was ratified (the amendment that ended slavery), Alabama, Texas, Louisiana, Arkansas, Georgia, Mississippi, Florida, Tennessee, and South Carolina began to lease out convicts for labor (peonage). This made the business of arresting "North Americans" (Blacks) very lucrative, which is why hundreds of White men were hired by these states as police officers. Their primary responsibility was to search out and arrest these "North Americans" who were in violation of Nigger (black) codes. Once arrested, these men, women and children would be leased to plantations where they would harvest cotton, tobacco, and sugar cane. Or they would be leased to work at coal mines or railroad companies. The owners of these businesses would pay the state for every prisoner who worked for them: prison labor. It is believed that after the passing of the 13th Amendment, more than 800,000 "North Americans" were part of the system of peonage, or re-enslavement through the prison system. Peonage didn't end until after World War II began, around 1940.

The 13th Amendment declared that "Neither slavery nor

involuntary servitude, except as a punishment for crime whereof the party shall have been duly convicted, shall exist within the United States, or any place subject to their jurisdiction." (Ratified in 1865). Did you catch that? It says, "neither slavery nor involuntary servitude could occur except as a punishment for a crime." Lawmakers used this phrase to create petty offenses (nigger)Codes. When "North Americans" (blacks) were found guilty of committing these crimes, they were imprisoned and then leased out to the same businesses that lost slaves after the passing of the 13th Amendment.

As a way to appease White Southern farmers and business owners that hated the 13th Amendment because it took away slave labor, the federal government turned a blind eye when southern states used this clause in the 13th Amendment to establish laws called "North American" (nigger) Codes.

Here are some examples of "North American" (nigger) Codes:

In Louisiana, it was illegal for a Black man to preach to Black congregations without special permission in writing from the president of the police. If caught, he could be arrested and fined. If he could not pay the fines, which were unbelievably high, he would be forced to work for an individual or go to jail or prison where he would work until his debt was paid off. If a Black person did not have a job, he or she could be arrested and imprisoned on the charge of vagrancy or loitering. In South Carolina, if the parent of a "North American" child was considered vagrant, the judicial system allowed the police and/or other government agencies to "apprentice" the child to an "employer." Males could be held until the age of 21, and females could be held until they were 18. Their owner had the legal right to inflict punishment on the child for disobedience and to recapture them if they ran away.

Racism was now established and perpetuated by

government systems. Segregation, Nigger Codes and Jim Crow laws were all made legal by the government and upheld by the judicial system; thus, "Systemic Racism" was born. Time to make a difference from the inside.

Now, this is my next move. In June of 1991, I began working as a parole officer for the State of Ohio in the Cleveland district. Man, who would have thought this was where I would land? The office is located in the Rockefeller Building right before you cross the bridge that divides the Eastside of Cleveland, where the "North Americans" lived, from the Westside of Cleveland, where the "Americans". Yep, this was the same bridge the C.O.R.K. protesters were on during the school strike when they were trying to prevent me from getting the education that helped me get this new job. I was now working from within the system and as a team, we were going to make things much better for all. It was a bittersweet assignment as one of my best friends, a true brother who had saved me on several occasions, Eric Ball, a Cleveland Police Officer, was just sent to Federal Prison following an FBI sting involving the Cleveland police department and gambling. My trust factor was at an all-time low so pawn moves are in play. No longer intimidated by integration, several teammates had no problem going into law enforcement as we no longer looked at them as the enemy but as family. Thank you, "Desegregation." I remember that morning's news flash:

23 CLEVELAND POLICE OFFICERS AMONG 47 INDICTED IN GAMBLING STING

THOMAS J. SHEERAN
May 31, 1991

CLEVELAND (AP) _ A federal sting that resulted in the indictment of 23 police officers on charges of protecting illegal gambling operations is "typical FBI grandstanding," a police union official says.

The officers, indicted with 24 other people, were suspended and ordered to appear today at disciplinary hearings.

Mayor Michael R. White says the indictments, which were unsealed Thursday and include seven former officers, show that wrongdoing by city employees won't be tolerated.

The "D.E.A.D"s had gotten my boy. Funny thing was he was just taking the overtime jobs that were being posted on the board at work. This had me very cautious while I went through the process of joining Law Enforcement. One of the perks of law enforcement was the concealed carry of a firearm.

Man, oh man, the paranoid thoughts that come along with this, and I get shot. "The "Dead" put one right in my chest.

Now, while all of that was going on, my not-so-typical loving marriage was good for the wand making it into the chamber of secrets and I was blessed with my firstborn on August 27, 1991. Ashley was just a happy go lucky baby. This was my girl. Me and Kim were both working crazy hours and would need a babysitter sometimes. We were fortunate that my cousin, along with some former students, lived in dorm Orr Hall, where our apartment was located and could help out as needed. I was very protective of my little angel and only wanted those who I knew watching her. The front entrance of Orr Hall was all glass and you had a clear view through the check-in desk. One day, I was coming home from work and as I peered through the glass, I saw my baby girl being held up in the air, then lowered down slowly as this student licked her face like a lollipop. I went ballistic. When Kim came home, she did not want to hear my side of the situation and before I knew it, she had called the campus police to have me removed. For me, this was the betrayal of all betrayals. She would have been better off cheating. When a person no longer feels or believes your greatness, that greatness which was the foundation to them being in love; then their love for you becomes that of a relative. The protection we have for the one whose greatness we believe in is constant and you fight by their side as they fight by your side for the purpose of the two of you being one. I was a "North American" with 85% melanin in the epidermis. Ok, visualize what that looks like. Quick science lesson so you don't curse at me.

Melanin is a natural pigment that determines the color of skin, hair, eyes, and other parts of living organisms.

Now, I am armed in a college dorm room full of extremely low melanin epidermis folks with several low melanin epidermis police officers on their way to deal with me per a spouse. There is that chance my life could be taken. What is the chess move in this situation? Remove yourself from that danger. I did and never went back. My first and only child was now without a father in the home. This would be her disposition for the rest of her childhood.

My office was based in the Rockefeller Building of Downtown Cleveland, so East Cleveland, here I come. My own spot this time, not grandmas. Just happened that as I was losing my family, my brother from another mother, Dennis, was starting his. Then it happened, the impact that is still with me today. The "D.E.A.D." had shot me again. So, I crawled home to the Eastside of Cleveland.

The one thing that separated me from my maternal family was the relationship I had with my best friend, Dennis Felton and his family. They were a mainstay in the historic Glennville area of Cleveland. This relationship with the Felton-Adams family showed me some values that would become the mainstay of my life. It's funny how you feel one way about folks who have no idea how much you really love them and the impact they have had on your life. The Adams family was heaven-sent for me and without them, I know I would not be here today. But they have no clue whatsoever.

Dennis is going to marry his high school sweetheart, Catalina. Now, this relationship is without a doubt the result of "Desegregation," for without it, they would have never met. If they don't meet, I am not here as I would have missed one of the greatest gifts next to life itself. They have decided to get married and of course, I head over to do my part. Now, I am not giving the loneliness of Mr. Pickle any credit for my feelings at that moment, but when I opened the door to the Felton home, I had the most fulfilling moment of my life when I laid eyes on their cousin Nicky Adams. Ohhh, my God. Now, in the past, I would hear them talk on occasion about a cousin who was a model out in California and this was her. To make things worse, we both were stuck gazing at each other in front of everyone before I could greet folks. Instant, and I mean INSTANT connection.

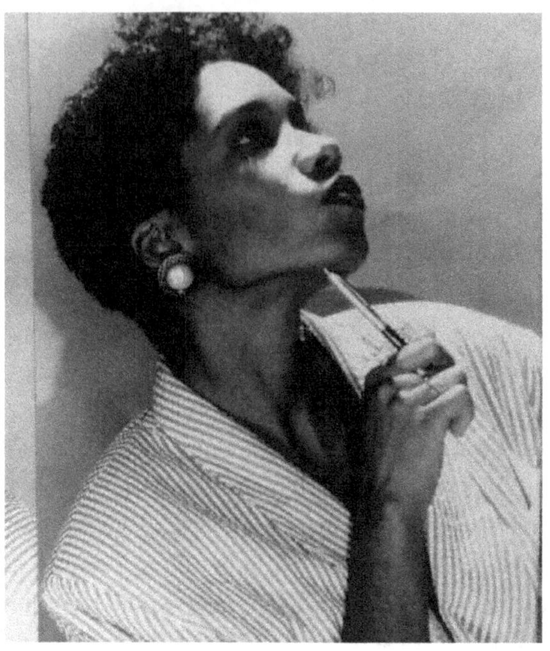

Here lies the problem: the family was still under the impression I lived in Akron with my wife, Kim. It's time to eat and we can't stop looking at each other. It's time to load the cars for rehearsal, can't stop looking at each other. Rehearsal, can't stop looking at each other. After the rehearsal, it was party time and the opportunity presented itself for both of us. Man, want to talk about the dam overflowing. She was going through a breakup as well as she caught her fiance cheating on her. She was faced with issues that were similar to mine in that her whole family did not know and were fond of this dude, just as mine was fond of Kim. She said his name was Larry, too, but that did not bother her. No one saw the two of us again for about 12 hours, just a couple of hours before the wedding.

Now, weddings are funny. They have a way of settling a person's heart. Everything in life had a purpose now and I found myself justifying all the negative things of late as what was needed to lead me to my love for the rest of my life. Yep, just that quick and based on her immediate action, I was hers. She had to go back to Cali to clean things up, though. After the wedding, we spent as much time as we could steal being together. The plan was set, and then here comes the call. It appeared obvious to members of her family that the old school "Ferg" had struck. I think they may have felt disrespected based on what they thought my relationship disposition was, so they called the fiancee. Somehow, he reaches us on the phone. She told exactly what was going on, and he asked to speak with me. Now, this dude was trying to sell me a story about how, as an actor, he has to promote himself as much as possible in order to continue to stir up opportunities. He really believed that once he got her back to Cali, she would change her mind, and he was trying to ease my heart from the heartbreak. So, I asked her again who is this clown? She reminded me that his name was Larry B. Scott from the movie, Revenge of the Nerds. I would have never thought this nerd's revenge would be on me. He was right, she never returned and I was shot with loneliness once again.

MY FAMILY'S KEEPER

To combat my recent spell of loneliness, I reunited with my cousins on my dad's side of the family. It was cool and my cousin James was going through the same thing I was with his spouse, so we decided to room together. Before you knew it, about nine of us cousins were hitting the nightlife strong. We had a lot of similarities in life that I was aware of but he may not have known. The most impactful one was the relationship we had with grandfathers. Just as I had to bathe and nurse grandad James on my mother's side, he had to bathe and nurse grandad James on my father's side. We drove the same types of cars, rode motorcycles and accepted nothing less than success. Although I was born first, he is the fourth James in succession as far as our family was concerned and I felt an obligation to make sure he was protected. Man did we party; it was a good time married with the start of careers and new searches for love.

You know, finding love ain't always about that first glance or that perfect body, nah. Sometimes it's about the crazy stuff we got to go through, like tossing a hotdog down the hallway – you know what I mean? That's part of the journey! So, on June

22, 1993, that hotdog produced my second child, Jean Marie, into this world. Man, she was like my mini-me, my identical twin, a real blessing straight from the heart, full of that good ol' LOVE for a lifetime. So yeah, I found it. Now, let's just kick back and let me do what I got to do, you feel me.

The start of my career could not have come at a more tense period since the civil rights movement. The competition for jobs was not very strong as we had lost a huge portion of our population to the HIV and Crack Cocaine epidemics of the 80s. It was a violent time, though. And violent times are bullets for the "D.E.A.D." A pivotal one was still brewing.

Ok, I have to go back a year or so to set the stage. Shortly before 10:00 a.m. on Saturday, March 16, 1991, this 15-year-old "North American" girl Latasha Harlins entered a store in her hood. The owner, a Korean dude named Ja Du, said he observed Latasha putting a $1.79 bottle of orange juice in her backpack. Du claimed to have asked Latasha if she intended to pay for the orange juice, to which Du claimed Latasha responded, "What orange juice?"

Two eyewitnesses, a 9-year-old Ismail Ali and his 13-year-old sister Lakeshia Combs disputed that claim, saying that Du immediately accused Latasha of trying to steal when Latasha had told him she was going to pay for it. A videotape showed Ja Du grabbing Latasha by her sweater then proceeded to snatch her backpack. Latasha then punched Du with her fist twice, knocking him to the ground. She then immediately backed away. Then Du angrily threw a stool at her. Latasha then tried to run out of the store, but Du pulled out a gun and shot Latasha Harlins in the back of the head, killing her instantly.

After speaking with the two eyewitnesses present and viewing the videotape of the incident, recorded by a store security camera, the police concluded that Latasha intended to pay for the orange juice with money in hand. The dawn of video evidence could not save Du and he was found guilty. However, the courts did not find that her life was worth more than $1.79, and Du was given probation instead of prison time.

On April 21, 1992, A state appeals court of California unanimously upheld Judge Karlin's sentencing decision for probation instead of prison for DU. Eight days later, on April 29, 1992, the Rodney King verdict was announced to the public. These two decisions were seen as negating the obvious, as the key pieces of evidence were videos from neutral sources.

In the past, the D.E.A.D. would take advantage of the out-of-sight out-of-mind and impose their own statement of events as being the most credible. "American" privilege is strutting around like it owns the place, even with everybody's eyes wide open to the truth. I'm tellin' you, this is like trying to carry a mountain on your back! Back in the day, "North Americans" were out here fighting against the HIV and crack cocaine problems of the '80s, losing so many good people along the way—now look at us, we gotta deal with this mess too? It's like every time you think you've conquered one beast, another one jumps out, ready to cause chaos! You can feel that racial tension all the way from Cleveland to the coast, and people are trying their best to keep their cool, patient like a cat waiting for the right moment to pounce.

Closer to home, eight months later, on the night of December 28, 1992, two "American" Cleveland police officers, Michael Tankersley and Jeffrey Gibson, spotted a car on the east side of Cleveland that had been reported stolen. When they approached it, a guy they knew from the past, identified as "North American" Michael Pipkins, was driving. When Pipkins got out of the car, he decided to run. The officers detained the passenger of the car, Rubin Smith, and requested he help them find Pipkins.

They drove around the neighborhood with Smith in the back of the car and Pipkins was seen standing on a nearby corner with a companion. When the officers approached Pipkins and told him he was being arrested, Pipkins did not comply. The officers quickly grabbed his arms and a struggle ensued. The officers wrestled Pipkins to the ground and Tankersley was on Pipkins's shoulders while Gibson was on his legs. Although the officers managed to handcuff one of Pipkins's wrists, he continued to resist and yell. At that point, Tankersley put all the pressure he could muster on Pipkins's neck and face. After about a minute, Pipkins ceased struggling. The officers were then able to place the other handcuff on Pipkins as a backup police car arrived at the scene. Tankersley and Gibson pulled Pipkins up, took him to their patrol car and proceeded to stuff Pipkins into the rear passenger area of their patrol car. Pipkins's head struck against the door frame; however, he did not react. He simply fell face down onto the back seat.

Pipkins's head was in Smith's lap while the officers left the area of the incident. During this time, Tankersley, Gibson and Smith noticed a fluid was coming from Pipkins's mouth. The officers soon thereafter decided to transfer Smith to a back up vehicle. They stopped to do so; Pipkins did not move from his position as the transfer took place. The officers then proceeded to the Fourth District police station.

Upon their arrival, the officers pulled Pipkins out of their car, dragged him inside to a holding cell, and placed him on the floor. Pipkins was not responding, so they summoned EMS. Another Police Officer, Deborah Miller, a former paramedic, came to check Pipkins and found no pulse or respiration.

At 10:23 p.m., "North American" Pipkins was pronounced dead on arrival at a nearby hospital. Dr. Robert Challener, Chief Deputy Coroner, subsequently determined that the cause of death was "cervical compression," or pressure on the neck. Dr. Challener concluded that the pressure applied by

Tankersley to Pipkins's neck area stimulated a condition known as the "carotid sinus reflex," wherein the carotid artery that supplies blood to the brain ceases to function and stops the heart. The fluid later observed coming from Pipkins's mouth as he lay in the patrol car was consistent with pulmonary edema, which occurs at the onset of death.

News of the incident quickly spread amongst the law enforcement agencies in the area. This was the cell phone era, so the vast majority of the city had no idea what had happened. A month later, our officers are going through firearms training at the Cleveland Police Department firing range. It was your typical live fire training that simulated bad guys. Like a high school cafeteria, the "American" officers buddied up together and the "North American" officers buddied up together. I guess "American" guys needed motivation for taking out a target and proceeded to call the target "Pipkins" and themselves "Tankersley".

What they did not realize was this is post-80s desegregated "North Americans" who were flowing through society like hot lava. Just too hot to be stopped. This wave was flowing all over the country in every facid within our country. It is a new world now. We hit the ceiling but chose to address it by filing a NAACP complaint.

Our primary office was located in the historic Rockefeller Building, which was also the home of Cleveland's great Attorney George Forbes and his firm. It only made sense that we take the fight to him. His lawyer walked us all through the process of filing a formal complaint against the officers and the department with the NAACP.

Once the complaint was formally accepted, all parties that signed the complaint were given a time and date to meet with the State of Ohio Director of Rehabilitation and Corrections, Reginald A. Wilkinson. The meeting was held in the lunch area of the building. After I have a seat, he gets up and leaves a file folder on the table with a picture of me in the middle of crossing the street on Euclid Avenue. The photo was sticking out of the corner of the folder- as if he wanted me to see the photo. It was clear that this photo was taken by someone who was investigating me.

Now, at this time, this dude was under national pressure as each day passed. It did not matter where they were and in his case, it was prison. For many years, the Islamic faith among North American prisoners was not accorded the respect it deserved, often dismissed as merely a gang in a struggle against white supremacy. Those who came of age in the early 1990s were shaped by the powerful legacy of the desegregation movement. They embodied a new resilience and determination, unwilling to compromise their beliefs in the face of misunderstanding.

On April 4, 1993, the tension between old customs and emerging truths surfaced with alarming clarity. The tuberculosis testing protocol involved substances that were strictly forbidden for Muslims—pork and alcohol components that violated their core tenets. Yet, the prison authorities refused to recognize the Islamic faith as a legitimate and vital aspect of their identity. The Muslim community made every effort to honor their beliefs, proposing viable alternatives, such as chest X-rays and other non-invasive tests that aligned with their principles. Regrettably, these alternatives were met with rejection.

On April 12, 1993, a plan for mandatory testing hung over the prison like a cloud, casting a shadow right on the heels of Easter Sunday—a day steeped in resurrection, renewal, and hope. It serves as a powerful reminder that dignity is not merely a privilege; it is an inalienable right that we must defend with determination and respect. On that fateful Easter Sunday, 159 inmates at Lucasville prison, many of whom practiced Sunni Islam, stood resolute, refusing tuberculosis testing. What began as a peaceful protest soon spiraled into chaos—the largest prison riot in Ohio's history was ignited.

Now, at the heart of this conflict stood Siddique Abdullah Hasan, the Imam—the spiritual guide, if you will. A man who, believe it or not, hailed from Cleveland, just a couple of years older than me. Over 400 inmates took part in this uprising, capturing the attention of the FBI and making headlines across the globe. Tragically, by the end, one prison guard and nine inmates lost their lives. The irony in all of this doesn't escape me. Here, we had a group that was shaped by the struggles and lessons learned through desegregation, now rising up to take a stand—even if it meant they were creating a different kind of division, maintaining their right to dignity for 11 tumultuous days. This moment reminds us of the complexities of our shared humanity and the enduring fight for justice.

T.I. Graffiti in L. block: Black and White Together 11 Days

When Mr. Wilkinson returned, I was quite surprised at the tone of the conversation. This guy really wanted to make things better and was looking for people to help him reform the State of Ohio Department of Rehabilitation and Corrections from all sides in and out of the prison walls. Shortly after our meeting, I was asked to be a trainer for this new reform. It was the cultural diversity piece. I agreed and looked forward to the challenge. The training was a week long and consisted of state officers from various state and prison locations. It was here that I first met this dude

Ron Stevenson. He was a brother from the next county over that had the smell of someone wanting to move up the ladder so I was really cautious as we still had our NAACP complaint in the works. What we did have in common was that we were both part of the graduating class of 1983. The difference was mine was from high school and he was from Oberlin College. What that let me know was that he missed the experiment conducted on folks by means of Desegregation through 1985. We could have a whole lot of differences despite the melanin in our skin.

Then he showed his colors or, for better terms, neutrality. The training wanted to produce trainers who could throw away the old racist propaganda associated with race and see it as it really was from all sides. When it came time to teach everyone about the status of the "North American" side, who do you think they turned to? It was the G.O.A.T., the man who got us going in the 80s, pudding pop himself, the one and only Bill Cosby. The primary training video was called "Black History Lost, Stolen or Strayed," hosted by Bill Cosby.

We sat together and while looking at the same thing, we learned two different things merely because of where we had come from. I still had the feeling as if I was a soldier in a war against the D.E.A.D. and was always looking to win that battle to stop the madness. He was a bit more political. This is still the best training video I have ever had the pleasure of viewing and I was told to duplicate this training with all of my Cuyahoga County staff. This sent chills down my spine. When I saw the year that video was made, a revelation hit me hard: Bill Cosby, that very man, had become a symbol of danger in this nation, especially in the eyes of the so-called "Americans" who claim to lead us. Now, let me drop a side note here—if you find the strength to go online and watch that video, you'll truly grasp what I'm saying. You'll see the broader picture, the implications that run deeper than what's merely presented on the surface.

The video was made in 1968 and clearly, the efforts of his life's work go to eliminate the wrongs identified in this book. He has methodically done so and in turn, pre- internet/cell phone era released an army of unafraid, free-thinking "North Americans" who are changing the world. From Oprah to JZ, Eddie Murphy, MJ, Tyler Perry, Magic, the Obamas and the list goes on. Cleveland was really putting them out from Gerald Levert, Halle Berry, Arsenio Hall, Terrance Howard, Macy Gray, Tracy Chapman, Paula Jai Parker, John Henton, Yvette Nicole Brown, Steve Harvey and Bones Thugs and Harmony, all "North Americans" who were reared in Cleveland's 80s and have touched the world. Through all of this I am still lonely and a bit mad because I am lonely. When will my cries be answered?

When I got back to Cleveland, the training was immediately implemented. Man, let me tell you, things took a wild turn after that. I felt like I was caught in one of those crazy situations—like, you know, one of those moments where you're the only sober person at a party full of drunks. My life was hanging by a thread, and it was no joke. I'm bouncing back and forth between the investigation division and the active parole division like I'm some kind of ping-pong ball. And let me tell you something, they had me out there making arrests with officers who were so clueless they couldn't find their way out of a paper bag. I mean, I found myself standing there, gun drawn, facing off with an offender while he had about 15 of his buddies lurking around like a pack of wolves. The tension was thick, and I was sweating bullets, no pun intended. And there's Gaither, my backup, running in with no gun, hand in his pocket like he's just on a casual stroll—what?! Meanwhile, the transport driver decides to do her best impression of a magician by vanishing from the plan. Now I'm out here holding this dude at gunpoint, and the crowd's like a mob getting ready for a concert, and I'm thinking, "This is how I go out?!". When the driver arrived she had the audacity to act like it was ok. Strike one.

So, I transferred back to the investigation unit. The second week in I got a pre-sentence investigation on a guy living in Shaker Hts., and they wanted it done asap. I had a schoolmate who was an officer there, so I made a stop on the way home.

He was out, so I spoke to another detective. After I gave him the details of the guy, his eyes got huge. There was a serial rapist who had been raping young girls in their homes and then making them cook for him before he left. He would threaten to kill their family if the girls told. They nicknamed him the Lee Harvard rapist. He showed me a picture of a guy who fits the profile of the guy I was doing the post-sentence investigation on. Then my eyes got big, I be damned if it was not him, and we had his picture posted all over our office walls for years yet his P.O. did not recognize him. How many lives could we have saved just by paying attention? That's another story. But I was feeling as if we really did not want change. Strike two.

BLACK HISTORY SERIES

BLACK HISTORY:
LOST, STOLEN OR STRAYED

HOSTED BY
BILL COSBY

By now, both child supports were kicking in and my check was reading $400 every two weeks. Man, I had two different courts fighting to get my money as if the other child did not exist. This was crazy so I had to get another gig, and that is when I met a brother from another mother. John Story was the brother of one of my co-workers and had just opened up a new jazz club called Sixth Street. The next thing I knew, I was pouring that liquor and collecting that dough.

I found myself looking out after John's back, you know? His sisters felt like my own, his mom was my guiding star, and the whole crew was part of this love fest working at the club. The town, oh boy, it was alive with energy, packing in every night—we were selling out like nobody's business. It's funny how life has its ups and downs, like a little rainstorm that suddenly turns into a downpour. The courts sorted out that child support mess, and suddenly, my regular paycheck was looking a bit more hopeful. Then John had this brilliant idea—he'd spread the joy by promoting concerts throughout the area. Everything was thriving except for my love life, which seemed to have gone on a holiday of its own. So, I thought, let's just focus on my two little girls, Ashlay-Blake and Jean-Marie, who have loved me through thick and thin. That's where the real magic is,

A big weekend was on the horizon. Some of the finest women in the world were going to be in Cleveland for the weekend. The Alpha Kappa Alpha Sorority was having an event downtown and the party was on. For some reason, I just was not into it and after work, I plan to go have a bachelor's dinner by myself and then spend time with my daughter. My office was adjacent to Tower City and they had a new restaurant called "Fuddruckers". This was a real quiet spot in the evening so I took a spot at the bar and ordered a basket of wings. Funny thing, on that day, I was the only person at the bar. Man can trouble find me. About seven girls come into the restaurant and with all the space in there, they decide to sit at the bar next to me. I still had my work clothes on and in those days, we went to work clean. One of the girls calls herself being slick and reaches for one of my wings while asking me for one. I quickly said nope. A moment later, a second girl asked for one and again, I said nope.

Now, in the back of my mind, I kept thinking about how lucky they were because had this been a month earlier, I would have put in a call to the cousins and my boy Kev and we all would have been playing motorboat tits and let's see how to make your legs look like wings. Get my drift. This day hit different, and I was on a whole 'nother vibe. I peeped the shorty way at the end, lost in her own world while her crew was just playin' games. So I leaned in, tellin' them, "Ayo, The girl on the end, let her slide right here next to me." They shifted seats like a basketball play, and she came over no hesitation. Man, I swear she carried that fragrance like a melody in the air. When I offered to grab her whatever she needed, she just smiled and said she was straight. But my eyes? They couldn't break away. She had that glow reminded me of every woman I ever put on the pedestal—straight-up, undeniable beauty right in my space like Diana Carrol, Diana Ross, Pam Grier, Lola Falana and Angie Basset. I mean a lifetime of women culminating with the last one to have my heart, Nicky Adams.

I knew from the moment I saw her she was going to be my wife. It took just one week and the help of the pudding pop man himself to seal the deal. You see, Bill Cosby was coming to town and I had floor seats. I was free, so why not take the model girl? Do you know she turned me down, saying she was taking her father to see Grover Washington and Nancy Wilson that night? I was pissed. The pudding pop man and I were being turned down. I wasn't about to make any hasty moves, so I thought, let's play it smart. I decided to bring someone along who wouldn't complicate the vibe. How about her best friend? So, I reached out to the girl who asked for my wings, and she said it was all good if Mel gave the green light. You know I'm fearless, so I called Mel and told her I was taking her girl to see Bill Cosby, but she needed to let her know everything was cool. It was a yes, but truth be told, I still felt a little heavy-hearted.

This chick really got my heart a little bit. We get to the concert which is at Cleveland's new Basketball arena. Our seats were on the floor so I escorted her to her seat and then asked if she wanted something to eat or drink. I leave her to go get the refreshments before it starts. When I got to the elevator to get to the ground floor, it was turned off because the concert had started. I then went to the escalator and it, too, was turned off from the down position. I'd be damned if I was not trapped and spent the entire concert standing two levels up by myself. While the pudding pop man does his work. Damn Damn Damn. All I could do was smile and say that was the hint and a half I needed to save my ass. The model chick is the one.

The next night, we met at Sixth Street and then went to the Club Mirage. There were long lines for both as they had reached capacity but we walked to the front of the line, and as usual, there was somebody there to let us in. It was hoping back then, for a minute, she thought I was a drug dealer because of the attention. But Sixth Street was my home and my close friend and teammate Calvin William was running security for the Mirage. Man, she was looking fine, wore this Pam Grier, Diana Carrol-style scarf around her neck.

I took a moment, breathing deep to find my rhythm. It got real, y'all. There I was, leaving her with the heavyweight king, Iron Mike Tyson, while I gathered my composure. When I returned, she was chill, he was as legendary as ever. She explained to me that she saw Mike often as he would drive his yellow ride to her best friend Karla's crib so that Mike's boy could try to get at Karla. But Mike was always cool. We had one more dance, and the vibe hit: the pickle said let's wiggle. Took her back to the crib, just vibing, talking it out, and suddenly I was caught in a whirlwind, her tears flowing like a melody. She looked at me with that honesty in her eyes, and I knew she meant every word. I was floating, no control, and then it slipped out—"Will you marry me?" She said yes. It was wild—less than a week back, I was just trying to enjoy a bachelor's dinner with wings, and now here we were, diving into forever. No testing the waters, baby, just a commitment that felt right that felt like destiny.

It was a beautiful thing, you know? Finally, vibing with my Mel and making each moment count. From jammin' at concerts to cozy getaways in the Poconos, we were all about that energy, even with the haters lurking in the shadows, ready to throw shade. It felt like our worlds were getting smaller, but everybody had someone who had their back. Danny was linked to my uncle Alvin, who was on his caseload, and my cousin Troy was the go-to barber, keeping us fresh in the office. Melonee's girl Tonya? She was right there with me in Parole. Danny, Kevin, and I were out there giving back, doing football clinics for Danny's son; it was wild how tight-knit everything felt even with so many souls around.

Something magical was in the air down at Sixth Street Under—John found his queen, Mary, and Kevin was swept away by April. Melonee became part of our family vibe, and just like that, we were reunited with Lillian Pyles, who used to shine in Hollywood with my uncle Billy Speed. And then, get this: my uncle Bobby was once the heartthrob of my supervisor, Sonya Kenyatta, back when he was making waves in the Rockefeller building, and she's still out here trying to catch his attention!

On July 12, 1997, we were married by the former President of the NAACP, Rev. Dr. Marvin McMickle. This felt nothing like the first time. I smiled and carried her in my arms all day long. Then we just kicked it like rock stars.

Before a pastor agrees to perform a ceremony, they request to meet for counseling. Ours was brief in terms of the concept of matrimony; but still going on the concept of purpose. Our union, the four of us, he, Melone, me and the creator, will last forever as its steps were ordered at a time we could not perceive.

This concept is really evident in his "One Life Can Make A Difference" sermon in Memory of John Lewis. So, we tried to live life to its fullest. We bought a boat and sailed Lake Erie, partied, went to concerts, plays, museums, fine restaurants, and road trips just kicked it till our heart's content, bumping and grinding at each corner.

This dude, Robert Patrick, from the movie Terminator 2, was from the Cleveland area and was filming a movie at home called Renegade Force. They needed some venues to fill the movie. Who do they call? Lillian, of course. Here we are doing a strip club scene with real strippers from sun up till sun down and all I could think about is getting home to my wife for nothing more than to hold her in my arms. Yeah, this was real. When the movie came out, me and John had two three-second shots; go figure but we were living the life.

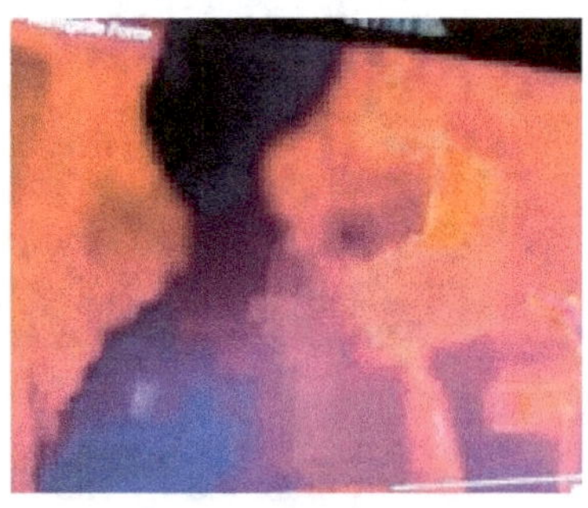

$$\overline{}$$

TOO GOOD TO BE TRUE

$$\overline{}$$

Sixth Street Under was nestled right next to the bustling headquarters of Cleveland's political elite—where suits and tie pins roamed like they owned the place. Naturally, it became the go-to spot for weary city souls looking to shake off the day's grime before heading home. Picture it: a bar filled with North Americans gathering to vent their frustrations while the city simmered with unrest. Cleveland, oh Cleveland —just when you thought you knew her, she was threatening to boil over, with whispers of the KKK planning a rally creeping in like a bad plot twist. And wouldn't you know it, our mayor —a real Tarblooder, bless his heart—stood as a lighthouse for equality in a sea of narrow-mindedness. Conversations swirled around me, and like a diligent detective, I found my thoughts wandering back to my real job with the Adult Parole Authority. It was as if the universe was playing a game of "Who Can Ignore the Elephant in the Room," and the stakes were higher than a Broadway ticket on opening night.

The North American male officers from both divisions began to bond. We used pick-up basketball as a professional learning environment for dialogue and planning to help with tasks on hand, especially violator arrest. We recognized we were all we had to keep each other safe in the violent Cleveland streets.

In an attempt—an endeavor, really—to align our officers with the particular demands of contemporary safety, the department decided to introduce pepper spray. A ritual of training was mandated before such an implement would be bestowed upon us; a consensus emerged that this would indeed serve some benefit to those of us who navigated the streets. Yet, what I did not foresee was the identity of the trainers nor the nature of the experience. It was, without question, among the two most unpleasant episodes of my existence. The D.E.A.D. and the gas.

The training unfolded beneath the watchful gaze of fellow officers, some among them vocal in their disdain for the cultural diversity training I had previously conducted. After the theoretical portion concluded—papers shuffled, words dispensed—the final act plunged us into the discomfort of gas exposure. This was not the controlled chaos of military basic training in the gas chamber, where instances of danger were meticulously crafted to ensure mere guidelines were tested. No, this was something far more peculiar. There I stood, instructed to remain motionless, eyes wide to absorb the sting, mere feet from a figure I recognized as a supporter of D.E.A.D.S, and then—to my horror—was directed to endure a deluge of pepper spray, unleashed upon me until the trainer deemed I had reached an adequate threshold of exposure. The experience left me in a state both physically and emotionally fragmented

Once we were all certified with the 9mm and pepper spray the violator task force arrest increased. In the past we would make an arrest just using two to three officers entering a home or place of work for apprehension. Now, we agreed to team up and we had at least six of us. Then it happened on a Friday. We got this house surrounded old boy who can't get out of the second floor stairway so he decides to jump out of the second floor window onto the garage and scales a fence. As I scale the fence chasing this knucklehead, I snag my chest on the wire at the top of the fence, then go to the ground and immediately come up drawing my weapon pointing right at his back three feet away about to go "tack tack". This guy clearly had an angel watching over him or maybe it was watching over me, as that would have been a senseless loss of his life. We did catch him later which validated how senseless that would have been. I went home that day and just held Melonee as close as I could, playing that moment over and over in my head.

The next day, I was at the club and this dude who called himself Andre Tiger Woods Sincere noticed I was not my normal self, and he invited me to come play some golf to just chill. Little did I know he was saving my life. I had never played but considered myself an athlete plus, he said I could win some money so I said yes to his skinny ass. Man, did that change my life. I was so embarrassed and broke after fucking with him on a Sunday. The next thing I knew I was either on the range or a course four to five days a week. After about a month, I was good enough to win a skin here or there and was now a course junky.

It's a curious thing, really. The North Americans lingering about the course were an interesting bunch—businessmen, former athletes, political figures—a motley crew engrossed in fervent discourse about the KKK, their impending march in Cleveland set for August 22, 1999, overshadowing all else. These Clevelanders, products of desegregation, were decidedly resistant to any notion of regression. Here we were, on this verdant stretch of golf course—some might call it the quintessential pastime of the American male—while they raised their voices in support of Tiger Woods. A striking moment, one never before witnessed in the annals of America.

The strength of that sentiment, palpable, resonated within me today on my home course. I refused to concede the fact that I was the sole North American in play, an insignificant detail in the grander scheme. This is golf, after all. But that's a tale for another time.

This was the last year of this century and it felt like we were being primed for a totally different world. We were being thrust into leadership positions of various proportions.

One fateful day, I glanced up, and there he was—Coach Jefferson, a pivotal figure in a seemingly inconspicuous moment that would unravel into something profound. He was there to interview for the head football coaching position at Cleveland Heights in 1999. As we conversed, it became apparent that he harbored a flicker of irritation. The powers to be seemed to like a youthful coach from Ohio Northern, a man with a wife boasting an impressive engineering background—a narrative that didn't quite sit right with our Coach "J". Caught in this intricate web of loyalties, I felt the tension between familiar ties and ambitions, but dismissed it, embracing the notion that perhaps everything unfolds for a reason.

As fate would have it, Coach "J" accepted the helm at Mansfield Senior, and from that moment on, they dominated the field. In a twist of orchestrated destiny, I found my way to assist Mike at Cleveland Heights as though I had been dispatched to this very place two decades prior, prefiguring his ascent. Little did we know, this convergence would also elevate Coach "J" and invigorate Buckeye fans across the landscape. By 1999, he stood as a finalist for the prestigious National Football League High School Coach of the Year

Fast forward four years, and in a significant turn of events, Ohio State's head coach, Jim Tressel, appointed him as Director of Football Operations, a role that would culminate in national championships. Meanwhile, I was weaving my own narrative at Cleveland Heights alongside Mike. The irony struck me profoundly—the world had contracted, revealing the intricacies of fate and influence, an elegant tapestry of coincidence that shaped our lives in ways we could scarcely comprehend.

I was torn into a minimum of five(5) leadership directions. I was selected as one of the union negotiators for the upcoming contract, and I became offensive coordinator for the Cleveland Heights High School Football team, On July 5, 2000, I became a father for the third time, and the real estate rehab gig was hopping, then Sixth Street Jazz Club and I also began to manage an all-girls band. All while still working the streets of Cuyahoga County as a parole officer. With so much going on, you know it was time for the D.E.A.D.

On August 22, 2000, Ron Stevenson took the reins as the regional director for the Cleveland Region of the Adult Parole

Authority. Now, let me tell you, this man was no ordinary politician; he had the finesse to weave through the murky waters of power in a way I simply could not.

A silent war was brewing, cold as ice, while I stood firm in my plea for the parole officers to rise, to strike against the paltry pay raise and the insidious drug testing measures that shackled them. Meanwhile, we were dealing with a new felony law designed with young North American men in its crosshairs, something they called "Community Control." This term masked a sinister reality—if convicted, a young man could wear that label of Felon and only serve six months behind bars. Yet those six months were just a stepping stone, a ticket to a revolving door of incarceration that seemed predefined for financial gain for others.

On the day I returned to Cleveland, seeking to ignite the courage in those officers, Governor Voinovich was strutting through the halls. My mind raced, fueled with indignation, and all I could think was one word: "Peonage." This wasn't just about policy; it was about our people, their lives, their futures —ensnared in a system designed to keep them trapped.

While in elementary school I learned of the history of

"Peonage" while preparing for a black history day speech. What surprises me is the number of people our society keeps in the dark about such issues as I remember it. Peonage is an example of systemic racism - Racism established and perpetuated by government systems. Slavery was made legal by the U.S. Government. Segregation, Nigger Codes, Jim Crow and peonage were all made legal by the government and upheld by the judicial system. These acts of racism were built into the system, which is where the term "Systemic Racism" is derived. The problem with the one that took place in America was their rationale in regard to the slaves. They justified it by saying they were not human and pasted analogies of the slaves to that of, i.e., lazy, dumb, without religion. In opposition, the stance was taken

"We shall overcome someday." I hear the music. "In 1866, one year after the 13 Amendment was ratified (the amendment that ended slavery), Alabama, Texas, Louisiana, Arkansas, Georgia, Mississippi, Florida, Tennessee, and South Carolina began to lease out convicts for labor (peonage). This made the business of arresting "North Americans" (Blacks) very lucrative, which is why hundreds of White men were hired by these states as police officers. Their primary responsibility was to search out and arrest these "North Americans" who were in violation of Nigger (black) codes. Once arrested, these men, women and children would be leased to plantations where they would harvest cotton, tobacco, and sugar cane. Or they would be leased to work at coal mines or railroad companies. The owners of these businesses would pay the state for every prisoner who worked for them; prison labor. It is believed that after the passing of the 13th Amendment, more than 800,000 "North Americans" were part of the system of peonage, or re-enslavement through the prison system. Peonage didn't end until after World War II began, around 1940.

As I remember, the 13th Amendment declared that

"Neither slavery nor involuntary servitude, except as a punishment for crime whereof the party shall have been duly convicted, shall exist within the United States, or any place subject to their jurisdiction." (Ratified in 1865) Lawmakers used this phrase to make petty offenses crimes. When "North Americans" (blacks) were found guilty of committing these crimes, they were imprisoned and then leased out to the same businesses that lost slaves after the passing of the 13th Amendment. This system of convict labor is called peonage.

In Louisiana, it was illegal for a Black man to preach to Black congregations without special permission in writing from the president of the police. If caught, he could be arrested and fined. If he could not pay the fines, which were unbelievably high, he would be forced to work for an individual or go to jail or prison, where he would work until his debt was paid off. If a Black person did not have a job, he or she could be arrested and imprisoned on the charge of vagrancy or loitering.

In South Carolina, if the parent of a "North American" child was considered vagrant, the judicial system allowed the police and/or other government agencies to "apprentice" the child to an "employer". Males could be held until the age of 21, and females could be held until they were 18. Their owner had the legal right to inflict punishment on the child for disobedience and to recapture them if they ran away.

How does this relate to my endeavor? On the day I returned to Cleveland to confront the impasse in our union negotiations, my mind was burdened with a profound awareness of how deeply entrenched our struggles are within the framework of our government systems. It was the United States Government that sanctioned slavery, that enshrined segregation, Nigger Codes, Jim Crow, and peonage into law, upheld fiercely by our judicial institutions. These actions form a network—a system if you will—hence the term "Systemic

Racism." As I stood there, I recognized that I was contributing to a continuation of injustices that would adversely affect countless North Americans. It is now my solemn obligation to effect change from within.

The following week, I was told that because of the merger of offices, I would not have an office within the State Building, and was told to work out of an issued piece of new technology called the Nextel phone. While I was in the negotiation meetings there was a firearms recertification class offered. I was unable to take the class and as such, was told to turn in my handgun. The weapon in question was procured by my own hand, thus the only articles that were seized were the very bullets intended for it.

I felt an insidious plot was underway, one that sought to extinguish my existence. Day after day, I find myself amongst those who have made grave mistakes, living within the shadows, armed with little more than a Nextel radio to sustain my connection to the world. Yet, in the solitude of these moments, I sought to uplift those band girls, guiding them towards a brighter path. My early mornings became a time of reflection, devoted to the essential work of parole, believing that the forces against me, the D.E.A.D., had indeed marked me as their target. In light of this oppressive weight, I chose to embrace respite and was introduced to the noble game of golf —a pause in the storm of life, seeking tranquility in the midst of turmoil.

IT'S MY TURN

A little over a year earlier, Pops had passed. Some say his girlfriend snuck him a cigarette in the hospital after days of begging for it. Before he knew it, he was gone. Part of my tribute to him was naming my son after the name those who came to know him called him "Dewch". This kid had stone eyes, so Maveric Dewch-Stone Ferguson was introduced to the world. It's my turn to break the cycle. The creator has done some wonderful things on December 30th. On this day he gave us both goats "Tiger Woods" and "Lebron James" He then gave me my only son on that special day. Maveric Dewch-Stone Ferguson. But my dumb as let the D.E.A.D. take a shot at us, and he was only one day old.

You see, the very next day was New Year's Eve, and I had lined up this amazing gig for the girls' band in Columbus, Ohio, at Mike's uncle's club. All night long, my heart was heavy thinking about my wife and son, 100 miles away, welcoming the new year without me. That was the moment when it all became too much to bear. So that morning, I had the limo drop me straight at the hospital— it felt like a scene from a movie, all quiet, like a ghost town. I knew both my queen and my little prince had done their business, so I felt it was safe to take them home. But they just wouldn't let me bring him out! You know me, though—I couldn't wait any longer. I asked to hold my son; he was my flesh and blood. They finally saw it my way and started to walk out. They actually tried to stop me from taking my blood home. After about 15 minutes of arguing they asked if I would sign a waiver for the hospital, I signed all the paperwork I needed to. Just like that, we were out of there, ready to start our own year together. A couple of days later I was reading about babies being stolen from that hospital over that weekend.

A whole lot of shit was going through my head. I realized what I thought was good was an illusion, just a lot of shit that was too good to be true. I just needed a break and was on maternity leave so in January of 2002 I took a trip with some Masons to Orlando. This trip launched me into that realm my father was placed in by the D.E.A.D. on the day I was born. Now, it's time to fight. While on that trip, we went golfing at a place called the Casselberry Golf Course in Casselberry, Florida. I happened to slice my driver out of bounds and when I went to retrieve my ball I saw some construction workers setting cinder blocks for a home right on the course... I asked the guys how much the home cost, and to my surprise they said a little over $100,000 dollars. I thought they were joking with me, and I asked again, "You want $100k for a brick house on the golf course?" He again replied "Yes." I could not think about golf for the rest of the trip.

When I was a child, my father talked about this dude named Willis who was paraded around as a mark of success. To follow his model was clearly in opposition to what a "North American" needed to do in order to hold off the bullets of the "D.E.A.D. who sought to dismantle the "North American" family. I was sitting in a great position to be the model Willis had set in Cleveland in the early 70s. I had money, women if I wanted, recreational time, an all-girls band, respect, and property, ran throughout the streets of Cleveland Ohio with no worry and a huge ego. By this time I had dreads down to my shoulders. I was on the verge of investing in several businesses. It looked fantastic.

On my son's second day on earth, I looked into his eyes, no disrespect to my girls, but I broke my own heart when I thought about how I let the "D.E.A.D." take a shot at him and he was not even a day old. How could he even know he was to duck the shot? It was me. I was the 9mm handgun they used to take the shot, leaving him and my wife all alone for this Mr. Willis bullshit.

I came to the profound realization that the paramount

importance of family needed to take precedence over all else entrusted to my care. It was clear: a complete cleansing was in order. I had to move forward. I shed the weight of responsibilities: the job, the coaching, the so-called friends, and even extended family. The irony lay in the disbelief of those around me; they thought I was merely jesting. I submitted my resignation with a six-month notice. Cleveland Hts football had rising stars to boast, including the promising Kelsey brothers. Yet, I understood the sacred duty of following the Creator's design. It was time to list the house for sale, aiming to find a corner of the United States that mirrored the vibrant spirit of Africa. So I set my sights on Florida. By April, we secured our new home, and on July 1st, 2002, I loaded up the Jaguar, BMW, Cadillac, my U-Haul, and that classic red Fred Sanford truck, embarking on the journey to Clermont, Florida.

Now, 15940 Autumn Glenn, Clermont, Florida, was truly a

destination set by the creator in Lake County Florida.. When I began to search for homes, all my mind could remember was that the city I had played golf in on my January trip began with a "C". The first one I found was this one in Clermont, mistaking it for Casselberry. Man, I dropped into the Lion's den. My wife did not believe this was happening and forgot to get someone to watch the kids so that we could fly to Florida to see the house. I was able to reschedule her flight for the following morning but I flew in anyway. That night, I drove all around central Florida, eventually camping out in the car in an apartment parking lot till I could pick her up, then drove directly to the property. The owners arrived shortly to show us the place. It was clearly smaller than our Cleveland Heights home might hold half the furniture and definitely had no room for our grand piano. After agreeing to put down a substantial amount the owners agreed to a Lease with an option to buy a contract. It was done; we are gone.

There was a different Willis steering the ship. Willis Virgil McCall, Lake County's sheriff from '44 to '72—a figure wrapped in shadows, a whispered name that carried the weight of darkness. His reign, a tapestry woven with threads of racism and blood-soaked accusations, echoed like a ghost haunting the landscape. Sandwiched between two of America's rawest racial wounds—the Groveland Boys met their fate to the west, while the Ocoee Massacres loomed ominously to the east—he absorbed the lessons of cruelty and circumstance, like some tragic bard of injustice. The aftermath of his rule swirled around me, an unseen storm, and all the while, I found myself caught in the sights of this D.E.A.D.'s gun, the weight of history pressing down like the heat of a long-forgotten sun.

We closed the lease with the option to buy early, taking on

a mortgage in December. Two months later the Homeowners association began foreclosure proceedings on us alleging we failed to pay association fees. The plot thickened, folks. Property wars, I'm talking serious drama here. Enter Ed Moran, the big cheese at the association, sliding into my life like a snake in the grass, trying to barter a truce to keep us out of the courtroom chaos.

Now, when he found out we were leasing the property? Oh, he backpedaled faster than a stuntman in a car chase, claiming he'd gotten his wires crossed and begging for forgiveness like it's some twisted love story. But the old guard over at Willis? They weren't having it. They pulled the rug out from under him, saying, "Adios, Ed! Your presidency is as good as toast." So, here we were, a lightbulb flickering above our heads, thinking, why not go for co-presidency? Partner up! Call it a dynamic duo. And just as we set our plan in motion like a heist, the venomous snakes revealed themselves. They vandalized Ed's home, scrawling "Nigger Lover" across his garage like some cheap, nasty graffiti artist had a field day. It stung, man. Here we were, just trying to build a nice life—pool in the backyard, kids' room decked out, sharing good vibes, moral high ground and all that jazz. But that graffiti? It felt personal. It fortified my resolve; we were in for the long haul. All of the years of pre and post-sentence investigations for the State of Ohio were kicking in and I began to break down the Florida statutes governing HOAs and for closures.

Orlando Sentinel Cops seek leads in subdivision's racial graffiti

CLERMONT — In the small south Lake subdivision of Weston Hills, residents continue to wonder who would paint racial slurs on the home of a man running for homeowners association president.

The Lake County Sheriff's Office is investigating the

incident, and no arrests had been made as of Thursday, Sgt. John Herrell said.

Detectives have interviewed neighbors and plan to interview another man, whose name was not released, in an effort to find more clues in the case, Herrell said.

On Dec. 6, Ed Moran, who is white, walked out of his home and discovered the slurs written on his garage and car in red spray-painted letters, he said. Moran, 70, said he thinks someone was angry over his plans to run for president of the board with Larry Ferguson, who is black, and Daniel Rincon, who is Hispanic, as running mates.

Representatives of the current board said they are upset about the incident and want to see the person responsible prosecuted to the fullest extent of the law.

"We are very distraught," board member Rick Croteau said.

Funny thing though, my entire household was helping the campaign of another brother named Barack Obama at the same time. My kids were finding their way with a belief in the right thing all the way to D.C.

They even became sports fans. A cat I used to coach back in Cleveland Hts, he made his mark as a starting lineman for the Giants, he was out in Tampa chasin' that playoff dream. That was their first taste of the fire, and it hit different, all the way through to today. By the grace of God, they saw Barry lift that Super Bowl trophy high, and Barak grabbin' that presidency—like the universe just blessed 'em.

Representing myself I was able to overturn the initial foreclosure proceeding while finding a huge discrepancy in State Statute 617.0809. It was quite simple. The community had never had an election since becoming a board. Its three members were given initial terms of 1 year, 2 years and 3 years. When they failed to hold an election anyone appointed was bound to only the remaining time left of the person they were replacing. Thus, once their time had elapsed there was no longer a place for a board member. At the time of my litigation they had surpassed 5 years thus all terms had expired which made their appointments void. This, dear friends, was the very opportunity upon which we could call forth an election, and campaign we did, filled with fervor and determination, convinced by the proxies in our possession that victory was within our grasp. Yet, as fate would have it, the specter of Willis appeared. With funds drawn from the coffers of the Association, he enlisted the esteemed law firm of Clayton and McCulloh, the architects of statute 617.0809. Upon our triumph in the election, they swiftly pursued injunctions, compelling the court to render its judgment on the matter at hand.

After hearing arguments from both sides, the judge agreed with our premise. This made me extremely happy as this also could be applied to the foreclosure proceedings as the people asking for our home to be foreclosed were merely neighbors and not a board that had the authority to take action on behalf of the association. He ruled no one had authority and placed the Law Firm of Clayton and McCulloh in charge of holding another election. I win and lose all in one. Needless to say, I withdrew and sought to protect my family. Somehow, in 2009 statute 617.0809 was revised and anyone looking to use my defense could no longer use it. I often wonder how and why.

CORPORATIONS NOT FOR-PROFIT

2008
Title XXXVI
BUSINESS ORGANIZATIONS

617.0809 VACANCY ON BOARD

1. Any vacancy occurring on the board of directors
   may be filled by the affirmative vote of the majority
   of the remaining directors, even though the
   remaining directors constitute less than a quorum,

or by the sole remaining director, as the case may be, or, if the vacancy is not so filled or if no director remains, by the members or, on the application of any person, by the circuit court of the county where the registered office of the corporation is located.

2. A director elected or appointed to fill a vacancy shall be elected or appointed for the unexpired term of his or her predecessor in office. Any directorship to be filled by reason of an increase in the number of directors may be filled by the board of directors, but only for a term of office continuing until the next election of directors by the members or, if the corporation has no members or no members having the right to vote thereon, for such term of office as is provided in the articles of incorporation or the bylaws.

3. A vacancy that will occur at a specific later date, by reason of a resignation effective at a later date under s. 617.0807 or otherwise, may be filled before the vacancy occurs. However, the new director may not take office until the vacancy occurs.

History.--s. 44, ch. 90-179; s. 86, ch. 97-102.

2009
Title XXXVI
BUSINESS ORGANIZATIONS

617.0809 BOARD VACANCY.–

1. Except as provided in s. 617.0808(1)(f), any vacancy occurring on the board of directors may be filled by the affirmative vote of the majority of the remaining

directors, even though the remaining directors constitute less than a quorum, or by the sole remaining director or, if the vacancy is not so filled or if no director remains, by the members or, on the application of any person, by the circuit court of the county where the registered office of the corporation is located.

2. Whenever a vacancy occurs with respect to a director elected by a class, chapter, unit, or group, the vacancy may be filled only by members of that class, chapter, unit, or group, or by a majority of the directors then in office elected by such class, chapter, unit, or group.

3. The term of a director elected or appointed to fill a vacancy expires at the next annual meeting at which directors are elected. Any directorship to be filled by reason of an increase in the number of directors may be filled by the board of directors, but only for a term of office continuing until the next election of directors by the members or, if the corporation has no members or no members having the right to vote thereon, for such term of office as is provided in the articles of incorporation or the bylaws.

4. A vacancy that will occur at a specific later date, by reason of a resignation effective at a later date under s. 617.0807 or otherwise, may be filled before the vacancy occurs. However, the new director may not take office until the vacancy occurs.

History.—s. 44, ch. 90-179; s. 86, ch. 97-102; s. 29, ch. 2009-205.

This move to Florida, which was designed for more simplicity and peace of mind, just turned into a glass overflowing with water. After deliberating with my younger sister, we thought it would be best for my mother's health if she moved to Florida.

Back in the day, I was convinced that every move I made was like a chess piece shifting on the board, all in the name of making sure Evangelist Hermel Graham could keep the family ship sailing. Then came Florida, a place so vibrant it felt like it turned the sands of time backward—no kidding. Her grandson discovered baseball as if it were some sacred rite, and her granddaughter dove into the world of art, splashing colors like she was Picasso on a caffeine high. Next thing I knew, my mother was racing around town, shedding pounds like old skin, practically trading on her youthful zeal; folks were doing double-takes, mistaking her for my sister instead of my matriarch. After three divorce ceremonies, she was kicking up her heels and finding her rhythm again, and frankly, I couldn't have been more pleased. But the real kicker? The way she now connected with those grandkids of hers. She even hired an artist—because why not?—to deck out their rooms with murals, turning walls into canvases, a living testament to their newfound bond.

Rearing children should have a holistic approach and my North American babies got to see all sides. As the dispute between us and the property in Weston Hills was nearing an end they became aggressively frustrated as it was an eight-year fight at this point. I did not help matters as this was also during President Obama's first presidential campaign and the whole family was helping the cause. This was the first time that such a stand for "Blue" was taken in the "Red" county of Lake. We all know the outcome but what got hidden was some of the backlash blue supporters in Red Lands endured. We ignored them and just did Disney.

One day in January shortly after the inauguration I got a phone call from a neighbor telling me that a group of people in the community were looting my home. I immediately called the sheriff's department as I was driving home and I advised them of the call and that I also had a Mossberg in the residence but my biggest concern was that my children may get to their home before I do. It was then like Nascar to see who would get to the home first. First place was Lake County Sherriffs, Second place Ma and the grandbabies, and third was me. Man, ma was heated, giving the bigots the business. When I saw our household belongings all spread out in the driveway I had mixed feelings.

Once again, these bumbling, thick-headed folks clung to their delusions like a moth to a flame, convinced that their wishes could rewrite reality. Sure, they had their sights set on our humble abode, but even as the sheriff's office stood there, straight-faced, reminding them that the place belonged to me, they were still shouting into the wind, claiming the law was all wrong. It was a scene straight out of a dark comedy, where the absurdity of their ignorance clashed with the cold, hard facts of the world. An immediate restraining order for them to stay off my property was then in order as a storm was starting to settle in. They tried to smarten up and asked to place the belongings back into the home. With a smile on my face looking at my children's beds, clothes and toys laid out in the dirt I could not let them lay another finger on our property. I went inside and was able to recover the Mossberg from its hiding spot. Then the rain began and we went to mom's place. Man, I guess she was here for a reason. She just kept saying, "How could they do this to the children?"

On my way to work the next day, I went to the house to take pictures of the belongings for the insurance company and wouldn't you know it shit was missing to top things off these fools went back into the home and tore it apart. I mean walls, stairs, plumbing, toilets, doors, you name it. As I stood amidst the wreckage, it was as if a tempest, a veritable hurricane, had swept through this sanctuary we once called home. The desolation was profound; the very essence of comfort had been stripped away, rendering this place unfit for even the simplest creature to live in.

Upon the arrival of the authorities, the info from the security guard professed ignorance of my identity and property, a silence that rang hollow under the weight of such devastation. How could it be that a vigilant eye did not witness the chaos? The garage door, once a sentinel of security, lay in ruins, a testament to the turmoil that had unfolded before us.

In the midst of such palpable hatred and destruction, my heart was drawn to a deeper reflection. I remembered the adults who once stood on the Detroit Superior Bridge in Cleveland, their voices echoing with the fervor of protest against our right to education, against our very humanity. Yet, in my spirit, I felt the call for forgiveness. We, who had faced hostility from those in the Lincoln-West neighborhood, who sought to inflict harm upon us, are called to transcend that bitterness. For it is in love and understanding, not in vengeance and hate, that we shall find our true strength and rebuild the world anew. All of that because they could not accept that we were HUMAN. Desegregation taught us how to forgive those who just did not understand that we all stand together. I buried the pain of the sight of my kids' tears to move forward.

The next day I went to the home to retrieve some personal items and take pictures for the insurance company. The security guard they hired was parked in a car in the driveway of the home. When he saw me he had this devilish grin on his face that clearly said he was part of the D.E.A.D.s. I disregarded his presence, lifting my hand in a brief salute to my neighbor John, who was peering from behind his window as if he were a sentry. I had barely settled in, no more than half an hour elapsed, when I stepped outside only to witness John's head shaking in disapproval before he quickly shut his blinds. Nightfall began to weave shadows around me as I turned my gaze, and then I caught a glint—no doubt the barrel of a gun aimed at me. Stepping into the street, my eyes registered three unlit police vehicles, ominously silent. They were positioned like predators, watching their prey. One officer had taken cover behind the tree, strategically placed between my door and John's property. I cautiously leaned out, my heart racing, and shouted, "I'm the owner of this house!" as I flung my license out into the open.

The officer relaxed his grip, holding my identification while I surrendered my hands to the air, aware that the eyes of the others were fixated on me, weapons trained and ready. He inquired if anyone else was inside. I firmly declared, "No." He then sought permission to inspect my home, to which I consented, though I couldn't help but point out that this was their second visit within as many days. He appeared taken aback, exchanging puzzled glances with the security guard. It was revealed that the guard had summoned them, claiming armed men roamed my dwelling, asserting that, had they seen a weapon, I might have been shot down without hesitation. I had narrowly avoided another brush with death. They win, it's time to move.

In an effort to maintain my sanity, I went back to a catalyst in the processes that saved my life, "Football." I began to coach at an inner city school in Orlando called Evans. Man, did we have some talent? Coaching was like therapy as I was attempting to keep my feelings in check as I dealt with the lawsuits and all of the lying from the courts and that community. Fighting the court case Pro Se is a story in and of itself and there was ultimately a settlement offer that we agreed to.

You know, reflecting on my tussle with Weston Hills, it hit me like a brick upside the head: I was totally blind to the needs of that other half, the one that completes me, you know? Life's just one big chess game. From the very start of this chaotic ride, the divide between men and women in North America was the ultimate weapon. This eight-year slugfest over a pile of material junk? It's draining me right in front of my own arrogant eyes. I thought I was dancing around the bullets of the D.E.A.D. But let me tell you something—those bad boys are landing with a thud. You can dodge all you want, but life's gonna hit you, baby.

Winning, my friends, demands a kind of coaching that is relentless, a method that I've always believed in. Throughout my journey, I've found success—not just in trophies and championships, but in the lessons passed down from the hall of fame coaches who shaped my own path. Back in 2014, I had the privilege of teaching and coaching right in my community at East Ridge High School. It was there that I encountered a young man named Terry Jernigan. Now, Terry had almost given up on track, but I saw something in him—a spark, a potential, that couldn't be ignored. You see, Terry and I shared a bond; we both understood what it felt like to navigate our childhoods in solitude, yearning for connection. I recognized the weight of his struggles, living without the presence of his mother each day. But I believed in him, and he knew that. In that understanding, we began a journey together, one that would lay the foundation not only for success on the track but for a deeper personal growth. Because sometimes, it takes just one person to see you for who you can be to give you hope when you feel lost.

Success brings out the vultures, and they ultimately get a hold of him. This journey was a marathon, but the stars were aligning. The University of Florida had its eyes on this kid, but he was battling those SAT scores. Terry was ready to race in the Adidas Dream 100 meters, the ultimate showdown for the nation's top sprinters, all dreaming of wearing red, white, and blue. But here's the twist: the track was all the way over in Harlem, at Icahn Stadium on Randall Island, New York, on his last day to take the SAT. So I got him signed up to take the SAT at Columbia University in New York, and I made sure there would be enough time to dash over to the stadium for him to shine on that track.

I was driven by a fierce determination to lift this kid up, to give him a shot at a better life. I hit the road all the way from Florida to New York because he deserved nothing less than to shine. His teammate, Kaylin Whitney, was in the mix, too, qualifying for the same event—just the kind of sisterhood we need to keep the spirit high. While Terry was hitting those books, I was at the stadium, watching Kaylin bring home the gold in the women's 100 meters. Now, I needed to hustle back to Columbia to pick up Terry and make sure he had his moment to shine. Man, was it tight. Then I heard a familiar calming voice and a hand on my shoulders. When I was in High School, we had a riot right after our championship meet. People were running everywhere. The most calming sole with a bit of protection on his side calmed me in the heat of the rage. Ohio Hall of Fame Coach Claude Holland, who I thought retired from coaching in 2010, just happened to be in New York with one of his professional runners. He still had the kind heart to calm an old athlete, coach and friend. From a far, he noticed our group and gave a smile of pride that what he and Bump Taylor and William Hiedeman had put into play was working at its highest level. I guess we were charged with taking care of others. I got Terry to the race, and his performance rewarded him with a trip to Eugene, Oregon, to represent Team USA wearing the red, white and blue. While I was saving his life I had destroyed mine.

https://www.orlandosentinel.com/2014/05/21/out-of-nowhere-east-ridge-sprinter-is-all-area-boys-track-athlete-of-year/?clearUserState=true

Terry Jernigan knows the mistake he almost made.

A senior at Clermont East Ridge, he considered skipping track season. Running at Lake Minneola as a junior, his season-best time of 10.95 seconds in the 100 meters ranked him 124th in the state.

"I am blessed to be where I am right now," Jernigan said.

Where Jernigan is, is a few weeks removed from winning the 100 (10.51 seconds) and 200 meters (21.39) at the Class 4A state meet in Jacksonville after entering the season as a virtual unknown. He became only the third area boy to sweep both state sprints in the past five seasons, joining former Boone standout Marvin Bracy (2010, '11) and former Jones speedster Levonte "Kermit" Whitfield ('12).

Jernigan's best time of 10.35 seconds, which he ran in March at the Bob Hayes Invitational in Jacksonville, ranks as the nation's third-best high-school time this season. He also ran 10.36 at Lake Highland Prep one week earlier. "Running 10.36 was a shock to me," Jernigan said. "And finding out now that I am in a group with Marvin Bracy and Whitfield that is even more shocking. They are world-class runners."

Said Ken Brauman, Seminole's longtime track coach: "No one

would have chose him at the beginning of the year to be a double state champion. Based on the times he ran last year, that's an unusual improvement but not unheard of." Jernigan lost once in the 100 and was undefeated in the 200 this year. He is being recruited by major colleges, including an offer from UF if he qualifies academically.

Larry Ferguson came to East Ridge as the track coach this year after spending two years at Groveland South Lake and 12 in Ohio. His first challenge was to convince Jernigan to run.

"With the correct coaching, the proper training equipment and a good dietician working with him, which almost any major college has, he can run in the sub-10s," Ferguson said.

Jernigan moved to East Ridge's attendance area and played wide receiver and defensive back for the Knights. He hoped to go to an NCAA Division II or Division III school for football, but his 33 receptions for 574 yards and three touchdowns didn't attract attention.

Disappointed, he thought about ending his athletic career.

"I wasn't going to run this year, but coach Ferguson kept asking me to come out for the team," Jernigan said. "I am glad he stayed after me. It has opened up a lot of doors."

He will compete in the Golden South Classic on Saturday at First Academy and hopes to compete in this summer's Adidas Dream 100 in New York City and maybe at the Junior Worlds in Eugene, Ore.

"I tried to increase his speed and natural gait by getting him to run down hills," Ferguson said. "We basically worked on that and on his technique."

Brauman said that was a defining move.

"In the state of Florida, because it is so flat, not many coaches have the opportunity to do that kind of training," Brauman said, "Running downhill really improves his turnover [quickening his stride]. I don't think a lot of people do that, but it is a very sound concept." Nobody will have to urge him to run track again.

When I got back to the crib, my plan was simple: kick it with my family. You see, coaching all these sports back-to-back is like trying to juggle flaming swords while riding a unicycle—

ain't easy, and it sure doesn't leave much room for family time. Just when I thought I could finally put the phone down and hear my kids' voices instead of refs blowing whistles, things blew up at school like a bad comedy show.

Now, we had to put the smackdown on some real nonsense, like suspending a kid for making threats that'd make you double-check your history book—threatening to hang black teammates from a tree? Man, that's beyond messed up! And then, as if that wasn't crazy enough, kids running around pulling down their pants and giving their teammates an unexpected nudie show. It was like every five seconds, someone was getting kicked out of class. We were drowning in suspensions, and we need a game plan, fast!" Enter Ken Knapczyk, the new head coach, a dude with enough attitude to fill a stadium. When the school wouldn't back him for putting the clamps on a kid who was stealing—man, he just told them to kiss his ass! Next thing you know, I'm hearing he's down in Texas, living in a tent in his in-law's backyard like he's auditioning for the next big homeless reality show.

In the heart of this swirling madness, I find myself playing the role of helpin' agent for my principal, caught in a storm of change. And then, finally, it erupts. D.E.A.D.S strides into the spotlight, bold and undeniable. As this chaos unfolds, echoes of violence ring out across the nation, with the tragic murder of a brother, Michael Brown, in Ferguson, Missouri. The air thickens with tension as sides are drawn, and the streets ignite with unrest. Just two moons later, the shadows stretch closer to home; my dear friend Cleveland Police Chief Calvin Williams faces the harrowing loss of Tamir Rice, taken too soon by those sworn to protect.

These turbulent tides at home feel like waves crashing upon my shore, leaving me weary as days drift into one another, and I sense the distance growing between my wife Melonee and me. Desperate to bridge that gap and win back her heart, I step back from coaching, and together, we embark on a new chapter, building a house from the ground up, born from the winds of the Weston Hills Settlement. What better way to channel those newfound resources? Ah, but the irony tickles the mind—just a stone's throw across the highway, and we find ourselves passing the remnants of the old place, a bittersweet reminder.

Citrus Pkwy, Citrus Highland, was my new address, but oh, how blissfully ignorant I was. Go on, give me a kick in the head if you must, for I knew well what lurked in the shadows of Lake County, yet I chose to linger in the lion's den. Instead of its hopeful name, it should have been dubbed "Let's Make America Great Again Alley." I've got the heart to withstand these trials; I like to think there's enjoyment in the struggle—yet my wife, bless her soul, has been living through thirteen long years of this never-ending circus I insist on dragging our family into.

Ah, January 2017—what a glorious time to be alive, right? Three years of frustration wrapped in a nice bow of division. You know, a whole lot of Americans were itching to hit that rewind button. Trump—yes, the man himself—was now presiding over the circus. And let me tell you, this new guy brought out all those antique behaviors of the D.E.A.D.S like they were collecting dust in the attic. It was like someone found the old playbook from "How to Be a Moron: The Sequel." And then there's Bill Cosby. Can you believe it? One of Dr. King's soldiers in 2018 was tossed into the slammer just when we thought we were having a renaissance of morality. Mom, bless her heart, moved back to Cleveland to check in on Grandma—because, you know, family first, even during a global pandemic. Covid hits and the whole world has signed up for a masterclass in isolation. Fast forward to January 2020, and America's divided more than a couple at a divorce court. It's like we went back in time—only this time, there's no civil rights song to sing; it's just a lot of shouting and angry tweets. Welcome to the show, folks.

In the harrowing month of May in the year 2020, we witnessed an atrocity, a somber echo from our past, as George Floyd's life was extinguished before the eyes of the world. When I first saw the devastating moment, it felt as if I had been propelled into a time warp, urging me to seek out the grim records of the 1992 murder of Michael Pipkins in Cleveland. There, too, we found an officer, Michael Tankersley, who unjustly took the life of a man, emulating the same inhumane cruelty we observed again. It is incomprehensible how individuals, who should see a reflection of themselves in those they serve, could act so callously, convinced instead that they inhabit a different sphere, a separate existence from the people they encounter.

This brings me to a crucial inquiry about the very essence of racism. The denotation of labeling a fellow human as a "racist" serves fundamentally as an urgent signal—a cautionary emblem for those who might bear the consequences of such a designation. In the unfortunate reality we just faced, to be branded a racist carries with it a profound warning, a recognition of those who might act upon culturally ingrained prejudices. This is rooted not in reasoned examination but rather in a belief, often unfounded, that has been nurtured to such an extent that the bearer acts upon it without the necessity for thought or reflection. This very pathology allows individuals, including those entrusted with the mantle of law enforcement, to strip away humanity from their fellow North Americans. And we must ask ourselves: how long must we endure this cycle of dehumanization before we stand united against it?

Everyone had a reaction to the horrific murder. One person who had a deep disgust was a frat brother and NFL quarterback Colin Kaepernick. Now, this guy is a North

American to the core, but did not know it. In protest to the murder, Kaepernick decided to kneel instead of stand during the playing of the national anthem. Man, this form of protest took off like wildfire. It stirred the scene like thunder in the night, a perfect storm tapping on the nation's door while the "Make America Great Again" fam felt that weight, every knee hitting asphalt like a bass drop. You know how the youth vibe, they watch their heroes, take that passion, and run wild with it —football season is on the horizon, ready to ignite. Every game, home or away, we knelt, and you could feel that tension crackle in the air. Remember, this was the land of Sheriff Willis V. McCall, a champion of the D.E.A.D.s. Then came the aftermath—the school board's decision to take out Coach Tez, not the principal, but the suits in the boardroom. Yet through it all, love poured like rain from his former players, respect rippling across the nation. On that year's NFL draft day, Sauce Gardner, fresh off a dream of being the Jets first-round pick, made sure to shout out to Coach Tez, reminding us all of the real ones who paved the way.

You know, as I observed people kneeling, it struck me as rather paradoxical. Here were individuals using a gesture—kneeling—to express a sense of discontent, but what they were really doing was revealing a deeper contradiction within our society. This moment, it seemed, represented a larger narrative, a complex tale of identity and history in America. You see, the roots of this discussion are tied to a shared past, a history that has often been marked by both struggle and resilience. There was a time when the words we used carried weight and meaning, reflecting attitudes that are, in many ways, still with us today.

The origins of how we refer to those with high melanin/darker skin evolved through a painful history into labels like "colored," then "African American," and today we arrive at "black." It's a continuum, a journey back that loops around, almost returning us to our starting point. The degradation of being called a Crayola title or Spanish term negro/negra (phonemes substitution NIGGER) for black, meaning black, dark, raven and gloomy. With Nigger naturally heard in the mind of 1st language Spanish speaker during translation. For example, Historical Black College. In translation, for their mind would sound like Historical Nigger College. It's not just Spanish folks, I was watching a movie called "The Piano Lesson" starring Samuel L. Jackson. I had the closed captions on, and every time Samuel L. said 'nigga' the closed captions read "nigger". To the degree that it is understood that the calling of a Native American "Red" of "Redskin" is degrading, it should be understood that calling me "Black" or "Nigger" is also degrading. I am a "NORTH AMERICAN."Kneeling during the national anthem has been both a powerful protest and a painful reminder of the fractures in our society. It's a signal—not just of anger—but of a yearning for recognition, for acknowledgment of injustices that persist. And yet, as I contemplated this, I created a litmus test to enlist the thoughts of others—talking with thirty individuals from diverse backgrounds. Every one of them resonated with this understanding, validating the feelings I grappled with. From that moment, I made a choice—a choice not to kneel. It became clear to me that this action, while rooted in protest, needed deeper reflection. It called for a more profound engagement with the values and ideals that truly bind us as Americans, not as symbols of division but as beacons of unity and hope.

I put the litmus test to work with a thousand people, and to a man, it still holds true; thus, I am a "North American." The test is a simple one that you can do on your own. It's just a series of questions searching for two following responses. If you receive the two responses, then that person has identified to you their place as a human being on the earth. Now, pick anyone and ask question #1. Where are you from/nationality? Question # 2: Where is that located? Those recognized as human beings on this earth, whether friend or foe, will channel the two answers to a land mass. For example, Italians (Italy), Russians(Russia), British(England), Japanese(Japan), Brazilians(Braziel) etc. Some may have multiple locations with DNA grounded there. I picked random people and found that there was only one(1) possible non-human sector. This was from the group that had no land mass framework associated with their title. Their title had been given to them by those who oppressed them. They had come to accept being less than the rest of the world by self-imposing denial of the same factors as the other human beings. They have accepted being something out of a box of Crayola crayons. They were proud to say "I am Black" for question #1 of the litmus test, and when asked where is that located for question #2, I would be met with silence.

It is a profound genius that the D.E.A.D. employs its tactics of dehumanizing entire communities while they walk among us! As I pondered the first question of my litmus test, it became undeniable that the very soil beneath our feet, the earth we stand upon, fight for, and build upon—it belongs to us. We are products of this land, born of its finest elements, here on this landmass known to the world as North America. When they see me across the oceans in Africa, they will inevitably categorize me as American. Yet, let me be clear: I declare myself part of North America, a tapestry woven together by people from every corner of this globe. It is our unity—not our divisions—that births greatness; it gives rise to icons like Steph Curry, Tiger Woods, Barack Obama, Henrietta Lacks, Sevtri Wilson, Rachel Rodgers, Snoop Dogg, and Kamala Harris—a mere sampling of the achievements constructed by North America. We stand ready to tear down symbols of oppression, statues steeped in the legacy of the

Confederacy, but still, we permit the labels that bind us—labels like "colored." Let us question what the "C" stands for in the NAACP. It's not mere ignorance; it's a programmed response, a conditioned mindset that we must dismantle. We are not simply inheriting history; we are reshaping our narrative.

In this contemporary era, we find ourselves gifted with the remarkable ability to witness the ongoing evolution of humanity. It is imperative for individuals to grasp that this dynamic spirit has defined North America since the inaugural encounters among its diverse people. Each soul, regardless of gender, has contributed to this rich tapestry—from those who wielded power to those who ventured forth in search of opportunity. It is this intermingling of backgrounds that has enriched our nation and fortified our greatness. With my heart brimming with hope, I stand in solidarity with all those who share the bloodline of North America, praying for a future of unity and justice. As an advocate for the cause of desegregation, I hold the belief that true equality is inalienable to all people born from the cocoon of North America.

DEATH

You know, stepping into the role of justice isn't just about the spotlight; it's about the foundation of our ideals. It's made me dive deep into the truth of what cheating really means. Picture this: two wine glasses, perfectly full, standing side by side. But for the shallow-hearted, it's all about the loss, and that's where the cheating mindset kicks in. So here I am, feeling like my wife's lost in a world that's not just ours anymore. I can't help but sense that space once carved out for us now has multiple energies swirling within it. And baby, the ripple effects? They hit hard, leaving devastation in their wake.

It's the 5th of July, my daughter Taylor-Blair's 19th birthday and I was in a very emotional state. A few weeks earlier me and my son were driving from Cleveland back to Florida and as we were going through North Carolina the rear air-shocks on my Mercedes s500 went out. Needless to say, I kept driving but every time I would hit a bump the tire would scrape the wheel well. It's about 2 am. when it happens. Pop, the driver-side rear wheel goes flat. The vehicles are flying down I-95, and while I am taking the tire off the car falls off the jack and my leg is pinned under the car with my body leaning into the driving lane. I had to do sit-ups to avoid cars hitting while my son jacked up a car for the first time in his life. It's a wonder I did not lose my life or my leg.

When we finally arrived home me and my son told my wife the story. She looked at me, completely devoid of any feeling, just shrugged it off like it was nothing, as if to say, "Oh, well, that's life." It was a bit disturbing, you know? It took me back to a time with my first wife, when she'd called the cops, knowing I had a bit of heat on me. Made me think my life didn't mean a bloody thing to her, and here I was, feeling that same hollow space again. Just a ghost drifting through a dream, wondering if anyone really cared.

That same time of year we were gearing up for my daughter's big day. This year we were hoping to wrap love around her with a set of wheels. My wife, caught in the net of her own fears about our girl behind the wheel, urged me to take her out for lessons. It seemed she had forgotten my stripes as a father, painting me instead with the brush of neglect. It felt like I was a ghost in my own home, shuffling through a scene where taking care of Mr. Pickle was only for bartering. The night of the party, I was riding this wave of good vibes, a delightful cocktail of nostalgia and hope swirling in my stomach like a bad burrito. I mean, who doesn't want to reach across the cosmos of awkwardness? So, I burst into the room, and there she was—curled up like a little enigma, all cozy on the edge of our bed. It was like someone dumped a bucket of longing on my head. But then, that silence? It was thick, like the plot of a badly written sitcom. So, I just lay there, staring at the ceiling like it was going to offer me some sage advice, weighing whether to make a move or just put my heart back in the box marked "Not Today." I mean, was my affection worth the potential for her signature "not now" combo? It was a real nail-biter. After a stretch of time that felt like a haunting silence, I remembered the deal we had struck, and I slid in closer, hopeful. But, just like that, she pulled the covers tight, a wall of fabric between us. I could feel the distance, palpable and thick. I let a little time tick on, longing bubbling in quiet, before I reached beneath the sheets, trying to stir some warmth, just to feel her skin against mine. Yet she brushed my hands away, claiming her space, gathering the covers around her, as if the night was something to be feared instead of embraced. At that moment, all I could muster was a whisper—a statement of desire to fulfill our agreement, to bridge that gap. But her response was swift, an unyielding pull at her pajamas that signaled the door was closed. Infuriated, I lay there, a phantom of frustration latching onto the reality of it all; enough was indeed enough.

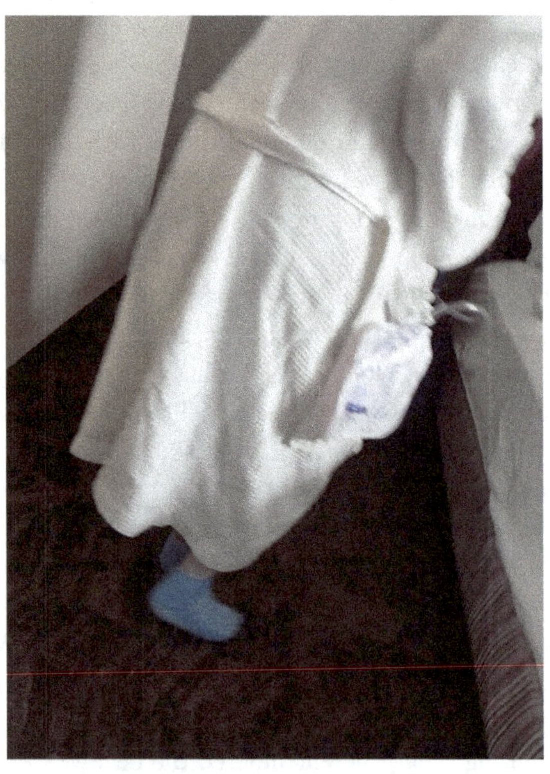

In my mind, I tried to trace things back to when it went wrong. Then some things started to come to me. Starting with her wedding ring. Melonee had decided she wanted a tummy tuck which called for me to assist with the recovery ie. feeding her, changing tubes and bedpans. Before going through the procedure she had to take off all of her jewelry. The bling and the weight—gone, just like that. Meanwhile, both her parents were fighting their own battles. Her father, Samuel Burrell, was the first to face the storm; 1200 miles away from me, he had a stroke. It was like the universe was calling her to step up, to take charge, to be the strength that he needed. All that energy I saved for me was now flowing towards caring for him, and you know what? I embraced that. Fast forward a few years, and her mother's journey took a turn too—dementia creeping in from far away, 1200 miles yet again. As she put her heart into caring for her, it felt like more pieces of her spirit were being drawn away instead of gathered. And the price? There just wasn't any room left, no fuel for this ride called life with Larry, my husband. It was a lot—too much at times—but I kept pushing forward, channeling that love through every challenge.

The D.E.A.D. just let loose a shot, man, like a thunderclap in the bitter cold of December '21. It's been five long years since my wife's lips found mine since love danced between us like a fleeting dream. Life, it wears you down, you know? Just when I thought we'd weathered the storms forged by those outside our doors, the fiercest foe rose from the shadows within our own home. Sure, my body still responds—hell, even a whisper of the wind has that old spark moving again, no matter the pills I take—but now we're reduced to mere echoes of each other, just the ghostly embrace of spooning. She doesn't see me, I don't see her, like two ships passing in the fog, and I miss the glow of her closed eyes, that warm smile like dawn breaking. The air feels thick, man. The TV hums louder, drowning out the silence, but underneath, it's like waiting for the world to crumble; if it weren't for the damn squeak of the bed, you'd think a pin would bounce off the stillness. My mind's spiraling, trapped by shadows—who's she sleeping with? That demon reared its ugly head for three full years, but in truth, I found peace, didn't care if she ran with someone else. I just wanted her joy, her spirit to be free. But just when you think it's hit rock bottom, oh it creeps up—now I'm caught in a barter of sorts. A trade-off like a dusty old deal. "I'll give you a little love if you..." You fill in the dots, my friends. The timing was a lottery, winning every now and then, but still, I held onto the hope like a gambler chasing rainbows, wishing we could shatter this spell, and find that rhythm once more.

I ain't no villain, you feel me? My heart beats for my family, but man, I'm worth more than this struggle. There's got to be someone out there ready to give me the love I deserve. I could only take so much of this heaviness, so I threw on my gear, ready to step back into the world as "Iceberg." I hit that club scene, searching for a vibe, a connection, something fresh. But as I cruised down the block, rage started bubbling up inside me—going to a club to find a woman? At fifty-something, after twenty-five years with the same ride-or-die? Nah, man, I can't let her choices lead me into their trap, the dead-end life they want for me. So I took a hard turn back home, stormed up those stairs, like, "Yo, we need to sit down and break this down." I could sense the resentment dripping from her voice, that ghetto fabulous tone ready to explode. But we had reached a breaking point, and it was time to lay it all out.

I was spinning out of control, a shadow of my former self, caught in a whirlwind of confusion. "What the hell is going on?" I asked, my voice tinged with a tremor, but her answer struck like lightning, leaving me reeling. "I don't want you," she said, and I could only manage a bewildered "what." Then came the rest, words flowing like a river: "This is just for you, I can't have your dick inside me. It's like a ghost of pleasure that doesn't exist anymore—my body's gone and closed that door." Alright, so you're chasing someone else, I shot back, quick as a flash. But she shook her head like a wandering minstrel lost in thought, "No, it's not that. I don't even know what I want these days. I could win the lottery, but if someone asked where I'd go, I'd just stare into the void." "Sure, you know you don't want me in that way," I countered, a flicker of defiance in my tone, "but come on, there's some kind of response down there, ain't there?" I couldn't help but reference the intimate truth of it all. It gets a little graphic, you know, like a song on a broken record, and she says, "Hey, it's just nature. If something slides in there, even Mr. Pickle, it's gonna get damp. Even girls who've faced the rapet—they might respond, but that doesn't mean they're asking for it." I'm caught in this tempest, feeling both shattered and strangely freed. I pull out a scrap of paper, trying to weave my thoughts as this storm brews. Is it just the essence of skin or the spill of her emotions that dances in my head? She lays it bare, "I don't feel anything anymore, no yearning to reach for you, no longing for a kiss or a hug, it's all faded.

Then the D.E.A.D.s question drips like a sticky tune, trying to come out of the shadows, the dangerous kind, "If you don't want my touch, I won't come near you, 'cause that's the ballad of rape. But if a husband and wife drift apart, how long can that play on?" A stretch of silence, and she answered softly, "Not long, honey. That dreaded word, the shadow I've tried to keep locked away, suddenly crashed onto the table like an unwelcome guest. "Us not being one means divorce," I muttered. She nodded, and it felt like an anchor dropped— she's no longer in love with me. With every note I jotted down, every slice of our life weighed heavy like a freight train in my gut. Every word penned was a nail in the coffin of our dreams. In the end, it was the truth echoing down a long, empty hall: she had slipped away from me, lost to the winds of time.

People, let me tell you, the pain I'm feeling right now? It's like a special kind of hell that just won't quit! I'm talking about that level of hurt that makes you wanna scream, "Get me outta here!" And what do I do? I went and turned into a full-blown drug fiend—yeah, I'm talking Benadryl, C.C., and a little H2O, all washed down with crown apple and a cigar like that's the solution! For my own sanity, I gotta lay next to her, but my heart's screaming for a break. I need to be out, out cold! Right now, this crazy cocktail is keeping me from thinking too much, but deep down, I'm scared, y'all. What if this is just the beginning of something uglier? I mean, the D.E.A.D.S are lurking like they own the place, and I'm stuck here in this dark corner feeling all lonely and blue. I filled my life with shiny distractions over the years—my baby grand piano looks great, and three sleek Mercedes sit out in the driveway, but it's all just a fancy mask over the pain. Nothing's working, you feel me? At this point, maybe checking out wouldn't be a bad idea. So what do I do? I go and buy myself a bad-ass Harley Davidson, start tearing up the streets like a maniac, hoping someday I'll just crash and all this hurt will finally come to an end!

It was four in the morning, and here I am on this bike, just waiting, right? Waiting for some car to finally decide it's time to pass so I can make a left without becoming a hood ornament. You know what? I said to myself, "Forget that!" This is my chance to stop the pain. I hit the gas and spun the rear wheels like I was trying to kickstart a motor. That flipped the whole night upside down. If I crash, hey, it is what it is! But that spiritual instinct kicked in, and I hopped up on the curb, dodging this car like it was some bad date. I ain't ready to punch my ticket just yet! But let me tell you, I'm fuming at these D.E.A.D.s and their crazy love addiction. Man, they had me hooked on this intimacy like it's crack! All this nonsense taught through neglect, blasted into our lives by lyrics and those flicks that show life all wrong! It's warped how we see relationships! Then there's this girl—I mean, she loves me like I'm her last slice of pizza, and bro, she really is the angel I didn't know I needed! Yeah, she's different, and that's the remedy God had lined up just for me! I feel bad, though, 'cause she lost that spark, that fire to touch and love, to feel that electric vibe when that special someone ain't around. Those feelings are golden, baby! But it's a double-edged sword, and oh, is it sharp! Only time will tell if we can cut through all this mess and come out alive. Dude, I was searching so hard that I could not grieve. Two people that I loved dearly lost a son and a daughter to that very vehicular act I exposed myself to. Dennis Adre Felton II gone too soon at 21. Son of my brother Dennis and Cidney Nicole Thomas gone too soon at 20. Daughter of my sister/cuz Kelly Ferguson. I apologize for such a selfish act. This world is not about me.

But all of this just made me think about why this is happening to us, and everyone that is involved. It all goes back to Pops. He would tell me about how the true problem with the lost values of us as a people was biblical and an international crime. Rep-oration from the United States would be letting the true thieves off the hook. See Pops believed we are a sovereign country as black folk. We are just forced to assimilate because our true homeland is lost. Well, I have evolved past that. Throughout my story, two true loves are spoken of sparingly.

For over 30 years they would lie to rest every night without me knowing their plight or them mine. They are my first unconditional love and harvest no ill feeling for being without me. How selfish of me to not see it is their love that has saved my life. Thank you Ashley-Blake and Jean-Marie for showing me what true emotional sacrifice is. You are the strongest woman itn the world. I need to fight for my life if only for you.

SAVING THE CRYSTAL BALL

Fathers are that crystal ball. When the D.E.A.D. would come barreling in, and I was just a heartbeat away from walking out on my family, believe me, it was that little crystal ball of my children's—yeah, it was that shimmering orb of hope that I was for them—that kept me grounded, anchored, fighting mad. For the first time in my life, I find myself devoid of a purpose beyond sitting down and writing this book. It's like suddenly realizing that every chapter written prior is really just one long, agonizing suicide note, and guess what? I'm the author.'

When I began to write this book, I was in a very lonely place. Scared of the truth, but the more I wrote, the closer I came to accepting the truth of my current reality. Man, I gotta tell you, it's wild how I've been chilling out more and more lately, feeling that stress lift as I finally grasp this whole idea of PURPOSE. Not just about me but the whole cosmic dance with everyone around me—family, friends, even those pesky foes.

It's been a solid decade of loneliness, flying solo, right? And let me tell you, that is a whole trip. Then, it all hit me like an epiphany during this dinner scene—just me, my wife, and our only son breaking bread shooting the breeze. I started laying down this wisdom, like a Tarantino monologue but less violent and more heartfelt. I was telling him about the journey to becoming a badass man in this crazy world. It's all about recognizing when that special someone, the one that God's got lined up for you, finally steps into your life. It's simple, really: just be the best version of yourself, and believe me, the universe has a way of working its magic. The two of you are gonna collide like two well-written characters in a script that was meant to be. Natural selection, baby.

All the weight of those frustrations and disappointments from the last decade started to slip away like mist in the morning sun. I understood, of course, that my children were the reason behind everything—my connection to something greater. Every day, every night, all the moments I experienced through my senses were meant for them, like stitching together a frayed fabric of our lives. It felt as though a huge burden had been lifted, even if it came with an ache, a sacrifice; after all, it had been eight years since I'd felt the warmth of a kiss that made my heart race. I slowly stopped counting the days since Melonee last showed me a spark of affection. We can't help but be human, right? Our eyes see, our ears hear, our noses catch a hint of the world, and our tongues taste it all. We need to embrace our humanity, with all its evolving emotions, knowing that vows and promises often don't hold up against what it means to truly feel.

Loneliness can feel like a strange kind of freedom, one that wraps around you like a cold blanket, but touch? Touch is its Kryptonite, the one thing that can tear through it like nothing else. The loss of that is what stung the most for me, stirring up emotions... It's the raw emotions we carry that shape who we are, a testament to what we value and how we connect. I owe a strange kind of gratitude to the Spanish/Europeans and pirates who were in the people stealing business. I am a product of your choices, and I won't be silenced. I'm human—just as deserving of everything every other soul on this planet has. I've fought back against the emotional greed of those who sought to strip me of my worth. I've claimed my identity, my land, my title. I am "NORTH AMERICAN," living this life with purpose and a spirit that is unyielding, embracing the joy that exists within this vast universe.

So, after we made the tough call to sell our place and cut ties, I found myself wrestling with that old familiar sting of loneliness and the hollowness of rejection. You know how it is —trying to find someone new in this big ol' dating pool. I figured, hey, I'm a North American, right? A melange of cultures like some kind of sophisticated blend of wine—but here's the kicker: I went on dates with folks from all over the globe. There was this Indian girl, a British gal, a Nigerian chick, and a Native American babe. Now, every single one of them had this chip on their shoulders, acting like they were above the whole Black American experience. They just loved to remind me that they were "different." As they trotted out the tired old stereotypes from the D.E.A.D. files—I felt my skin start to twitch. I mean, I wanted to scream, "Then leave North America and all that its "North American" cocoon has built for the comforts of your life." That sentiment was proof positive that the litmus experiment had worked. It also released any and all animosity I had towards Melonee, and I realized that all tension had faded away. She wasn't the villain in this story. So here I am, ready to fight for her, channeling all my anger towards those other folks into something real while packing the house for the move. Then, outta nowhere, Melonee. She hits me with this simple yet heavy question, "What if I want my husband?" All I could do was nod, one might say an almost tearful nod. Yeah—man, this was real! I'm here, standing solid with everyone who's called this land home.

In holding the belief that true equality is inalienable to all people born from the cocoon of North America and all her blessings, thus at the end of the day, no matter what shade of skin. The social construct of a primary visual used to justify enslavement and support the creation of a hierarchy of human beings uses a scale where darker-skinned people are placed at the bottom of the hierarchy. This is race. I am more and denounce the race primary visual as my descriptor... I am more made by this land, which is made of my blood. The complex concept of elements that is of uniquely blended shared cultures, from language, traditions, food, arts, ideas, heritage, common ancestry etc, has created a unique cultural identity that has been and continues to be passed down through generations on the land belonging to America. In sharing a sense of belonging to the country of "America," my ethnicity is and will forever be equal to that of other earthly humans. That is what gives this "North American the ability to fight on.

ABOUT THE AUTHOR

Larry Ferguson Jr. M.Ed., lives in Florida. An avid golfer known as a coach of all sports and, above all husband, father, brother and son.